MW01229327

PEN PEARLS

A Personal Anthology

By

SUZANNE DE BOARD

Back cover and Interior Illustrations
by Suzanne de Board

* * *

ISBN: 1478185597
ISBN-13: 9781478185598
Library of Congress Control Number: 2012912132
CreateSpace Independent Publishing Platform
North Charleston, South Carolina

To my readers.
To those who laugh with me, who cry with me,
and to those who simply enjoy these pages.
This book is dedicated to you.

Acknowledgements

S PECIAL THANKS TO my daughter, Christina, who has read everything I have ever written, and has not been afraid to let me know where I could improve. Also, I want to thank my critique groups for helping me to polish and prepare my book for publication — Ingrid Claus, Jim Elstad, Marilyn Ramirez, Mary Thompson, Denny Stanz, Linda Smith, Robert Foster, Evelyn Blocker, Winnie Rueff, and all those helpful souls who made this publication possible. And a very special thanks to my husband, Willard Brumbaugh, who listened, helped me research, and gave me much needed encouragement during the many hours, weeks, and months of preparation.

In addition, I would like to thank Ronnell D Porter, the artist, who did such an excellent job preparing the artwork for the cover of this book.

PEN PEARLS

Table of Contents

CHILDREN

CHRISTMAS/HOLIDAY

DRAMATIC

EMOTION

HUMOR

NATURE

ROMANCE

SACRED

SKETCHES AND OTHER PROJECTS

(Children's Literature Course Exercises)

The date in the upper left hand corner of each poem, and short story, is the original date written.

CHILDREN

A JOYFUL NOISE

"**O**H BEAUTIFUL, FOR spacious skies," she bellowed, happily unaware she was slightly off key. Her long braids swayed as she kept time with the music in her body. Kevin, her older brother, longed to reach out and yank one of those braids. *Anything to shut her up*, he thought. *Ugh!* But she continued to make a joyful, if not so beautiful, noise, to the consternation of those around her.

"Hey, loud mouth," Kevin whispered in her good ear. "Give me a break. You're ruining my life back here."

But she ignored him, tossing her braids in defiance.

Kevin grumbled under his breath as his mother frowned, placing her index finger against her lips. *Is it possible Mom's tone deaf*, he wondered? *Or is she just protecting her precious daughter?* As soon as the service was over, he planned to escape. His best friend, Jeremy, should be home by now and if he hurried, maybe they could make it to the basketball court before anyone else arrived. Kevin lived for basketball, so it was understandable that it was the place he most wanted to be. At last, the final hymn was sung and the benediction prayed.

"I'm out-a-here," he muttered as he made a beeline for the sanctuary door.

"Kevin . . ? KEVIN!"

"Aw, rats," he grumbled as he made his way back up the aisle where his mother waited, arms crossed, a deep frown creasing her brow.

"Where do you think *you're* going, young man?" she asked. "You know the routine."

Kevin scowled, and gripping the handles of the wheelchair began recklessly pushing his sister to the handicap van parked just outside the church foyer.

"And be nice about it," his mother called as he slipped through the door.

He skidded to a stop, narrowly missing the side of the van, set the brakes and kicked at the wheelchair. "There, your highness," he snapped. "Do I have your permission to leave?" But before she could answer he was off.

"Hey, Kevin! Catch!"

Kevin looked up just in time to see the basketball leave Jeremy's hands and hurtle towards him. Rats. It was too high. Jeremy never could throw. Kevin's arms stretched high as he stumbled backward to catch the ball before it bounced.

"Kevin! Look out!" His sister's scream reached him just before the squeal of tires. Then . . . darkness.

* * *

"Rock of Ages, cleft for me . . . ." The brother-sister duo sang lustily, Kevin's critical ear somehow miraculously healed.

"Hey," she whispered with a grin. "You sing worse than I do."

"At least I keep better time," he grinned back, tap, tap, tapping with one of his crutches on the well-worn carpet. Life was good. He wouldn't be playing basketball for awhile, but at least he was still alive. He was lucky . . . very lucky . . . just a broken leg and a slight concussion.

His mind wandered back to that Sunday afternoon three weeks ago, when he stepped backward into the street, pausing for just a moment when he heard her call his name. He should have paid more attention. One more step and he would have been history.

"Thanks, sis," he whispered, and then almost as an after-thought added, "the most wonderful voice in the world."

9/22/10

BLACK CAT-WITCH'S CAT

FELICITE FAYOLA LEANED heavily on the yellowed windowsill of her grandparent's home and sighed. Tomorrow was Friday the thirteenth, and she knew that she wouldn't be allowed outside for the entire day. If the truth were known, she wouldn't leave the house even if it *was* permitted. Friday the thirteenth was the unluckiest day of the whole year, and she did not want to take any chances.

"Felicite Fayola, what are you doing inside on such a beautiful day?" her grandmother asked. "Go outside and play. It will be good for you. Go on." She patted Felicite on her bottom and shooed her toward the door.

"But, Grandma, what if—"

"No what ifs," her grandmother said. "Tomorrow is the day for staying inside. Today is for having a good time. Do you have all your charms with you?"

"Yes, Grandma." Felicite fingered the rabbit's foot in her jeans' right pocket. Soft and fluffy and the whitest white she had ever seen. White stood for purity, and nothing bad could happen to you if you had a whiter-than-white rabbit's foot in your pocket. However, just to be on the safe side, a four-leaf clover and a tiny horseshoe were nestled in her other pocket. She wasn't certain whether the horseshoe was right-side-up or upside-down, but it didn't really matter, she supposed.

Mama said a horseshoe should always be pointed up, to hold in the blessings, but Uncle Andrew said it should always be pointed down so the blessings could be poured out on the receiver. So it didn't really matter. It was lucky either way. She carefully shut the front door, and taking baby steps, walked down the path to the sidewalk.

She was a brave girl, most of the time, and she knew just what to do to keep safe. She never stepped on cracks in the sidewalk, and absolutely never walked under a ladder. She was always careful, but sometimes, crazy things happened anyway.

The only thing she was truly afraid of was old Mrs. Willy's big black cat. Mrs. Willy was strange, and everyone knew she was a witch, but no one ever said much. She had only one eye, a huge nose with a wart right in the middle, and was often seen sweeping her walkway with an old straw broom. But Mrs. Willy's big black cat . . . that was the clincher.

Mrs. Willy made it her business to know everything about everyone, and *everybody* knew the big black cat was her spy, just like all scary witches have. Sometimes that cat would just watch you with his slanted yellow-green eyes, and sometimes he tried to act friendly, but everyone knew that was just his way of finding out things to report back to Mrs. Willy. So Felicite kept her distance.

"Hi, Felicite. Whatcha doin'?"

"Taking a walk. Wanta come along?" Felicite grinned at her best friend, Michael Cavanaugh. "Thought I'd go down to the park for a while."

"Sounds like fun," he grinned back. "But did you know old Mrs. Willy's cat is following you?"

"What?" Felicite turned her head just enough to see the swishing tail of the big black cat, and began to walk faster.

"Hey, where ya goin'? It's just Mrs. Willy's cat. He won't hurt you." He paused to scratch the cat behind his ears. The cat began to purr, rubbing against Michael's leg, but kept his eyes fixed on Felicite.

"That's a witch cat. How can you bear to touch it?" Felicite shuddered, backing away a few steps. "Tell it to go away."

"Who? Tobias? He's a cool cat."

"He's a witch cat! And . . . and if you won't tell it to go away, you can just . . . just stay here and play with it, and I'll go to the park . . . by myself." She took several shaky steps backward before turning and racing toward the park. She didn't even look behind her to see whether Michael was coming or not. Tears of fear and anger threatened as she slowed to a walk and collapsed at the base of the new swing set.

She laid her head against the steel post, cold and hard, but somehow reassuring. Panting, she shut her eyes and waited for her breathing to slow and her heart rate to return to normal. That was too close. What was the matter with Michael? Didn't he realize the danger he was putting them both in? But she was safe for now, that's what counts. But Michael. She should never have left him at the mercy of that witch cat. "Where are you, Michael?" she whispered. "Please be safe."

She crawled to the nearest swing and pulled herself up using the chain as leverage. The seat was hard, and new, not yet having attained the worn softness of the well used. She pushed with her feet, gently at first, then with more force until she could see over the top rail of the swing set. She closed her eyes, her hair flying loose and free. She leaned back, pumping and pumping and pumping the fear away. She smiled, breathing in the sweet, pungent scent of the fresh mown grass, and the fresh scent of imminent rain. Thunder rolled somewhere in the distance.

Merow

Felicite stiffened, slowly opening one eye. *Witch cat*, she shuddered, and began to pump harder. But where was Michael?

Me-row

She opened both eyes and stared at the big black menace. The cat began to yowl, turned and walked away a few paces. But when Felicite didn't follow, he ran back toward the swing, stood in front of Felicite and yowled once again. He anxiously began to knead the grass at the edge of the sand, turned and padded several paces toward the park entrance before looking back at Felicite, calling . . . calling . . . .

What's wrong with that cat, she frowned? Michael? Did something happen to Michael, or is this just a trick—a witch trick—of some kind? She slowed, dragging her feet in the sand with each pass until she stopped completely. The cat obviously wanted her to follow him, but why?

She stood, her knees wobbly, her heart beginning to pound once more. She would follow the cat, but safely, at a distance. Then if it turned out to be a trick, she could run to safety. Careful to keep from crossing the cat's path, she followed him out of the park and down to the next block.

"Michael!" she cried. She forgot the witch cat as she raced to her best friend's side. "What happened? Are you okay?" She knelt in the damp grass beside him, his pain now mirrored in her eyes. The black cat, skittish and wary, walked in a continuous circle around them, but Felicite didn't seem to notice.

"I tried to follow you, but I stepped in a gopher hole and twisted my ankle. It hurts real bad, and I can't walk on it," he moaned. "You need to get help, please."

"That cat! I knew he was trouble!" She clenched her fists as angry tears filled her eyes.

"Don't blame Tobias. It wasn't his fault. I should have paid more attention to where I was going. Oooow. Please, Felicite, go get some help."

"I'll get Papa. I'll be right back." She jumped to her feet, but her feet wouldn't move. A cold sweat engulfed her as she watched the cat circling them.

"What's the matter?" Michael groaned. "Go!"

"I . . . I can't."

"Why not?"

"The cat . . . ."

"Forget Tobias. If you don't go get help, I'm dead."

Felicite stared at Michael, then at the circle the cat was making. Michael was more important than her fear, so closing her eyes she stepped over the imaginary line left by the witch cat and began to run. Seconds later, she rounded a corner and ran smack dab into the witch. The old woman gripped her arms fiercely as Felicity struggled to get away, but the witch only gripped more firmly.

"Let me go!" Felicite screamed.

"Where's my cat? What'd ya do with 'im?"

"H-he's with M-Michael. M-Michael's hurt. I-I've gotta get help."

"Show me." The witch began to pull on Felicite's arm.

Terrified, she tried to jerk free, but the witch was just too strong. Felicite swallowed hard, said a quick prayer, and reluctantly led the way to her best friend. The old woman knelt beside the boy, gently caressed his forehead, and checked his ankle for a break. She ordered Felicite to help as she attempted to lift the boy.

Together, one on either side, they half-carried him to the witch's house. Felicite hesitated, before entering, but Michael was more important than her fear, so she helped him hobble to the couch and stayed with him while the witch hurried to find an ace bandage to wrap the boy's swollen ankle.

Felicite, ready to flee for help at a moment's notice, glanced around the tiny living room. This was exactly how she expected the witch's house from "Hansel and Gretel" to look. Sweet and sugar-plum-ish.

Pictures lined the walls. She stared at the picture nearest her. A pretty, young girl, dressed in princess-clothes, stared back at her. Next to the princess picture, an ugly crone, with green skin, and a pointed hat, cackled on a broomstick. The figure looked familiar, but she couldn't quite place her.

"You like those?" the witch asked, carefully wrapping Michael's ankle, but speaking to Felicite, her squinty eye now open and fixed on her guest. "Those were the days . . . in me prime." Her voice took on the personification of the witch Felicite so feared.

"Personally, I prefer the princess look, but my best reviews were for "The Wizard of Oz." I was pretty good in my day. Most people still think of me in the part I made most famous. Folks have called me 'the witch of North County' ever since. Here, have some milk and cookies."

The witch was an actress? An actress, and not a real witch at all? She glanced at Michael.

"Grandma was the best, in her day. Everybody said so." He grinned at Felicite, grabbed a cookie and offered her one. The big black cat slept at his feet. Felicite took the cookie, but glared at Michael, accusation in her eyes.

"Mrs. Willy is your grandma, and you never told me? How could you keep something as important as that a secret . . . from me, your best friend?"

Michael shifted uncomfortably. "I knew how you felt, and I didn't want to lose you."

Felicite glanced from Michael to the pictures on the wall, and back to Michael. *Mrs. Willy was not a witch, so her cat couldn't be a witch cat.* She shrugged her shoulders, gave him an 'it's okay this time, but don't let it happen again' look, then smiled and said, "Best friends forever?" And that was all.

* * *

Friday the thirteenth dawned bright, and fresh, and beautiful. Felicite was up and dressed before anyone else in the family, ready for the day.

"Excuse me, young lady. Where do you think you're going?" Her grandmother stood with her arms across her chest, glaring at her youngest granddaughter. "Did you forget what day this is?"

"Nope. It's Friday, the day before Saturday, and I'm going to visit Michael and his grandma, Mrs. Willy." Her lucky talismans rested silently on the kitchen table. "Wanta come?"

CHERRY

THE EAR-PIERCING WHISTLE screamed a warning, and Cherry's hands flew to her ears, covering them as tightly as she could. "What was that?" She turned to her country cousin, Sam, as he grabbed their jackets, gripped her arm and began to pull her toward the front door; the unfinished puzzle pieces scattered across the coffee table and onto the floor.

"Tornado! Come on! We've got to get to the barn before it hits. That's the three minute warning. Hurry up."

Cherry threw on her jacket and bolted after Sam. *A tornado? Whoa.* And she thought her summer vacation was going to be boring. Uncle Henry was wildly gesturing, and appeared to be screaming something, but the wind was just too loud. *Where did it come from, anyway, this explosion of weather? An hour ago it had been sunny, and bright, and still, but now . . . wow.* She glanced over her left shoulder, and grinned. This was so exciting. A real tornado and she was part of it.

Out of the corner of her eye, she caught a movement near the fluttering screen door. *Molly!* The little sheltie quivered in the doorway, a small bundle of fur gripped between her teeth, her eyes filled with terror, as the screen door slammed, flew opened, and slammed again. *Oh, no.* Suddenly this was no longer fun and games. Molly's life was in danger, and the lives of her pups. She turned and began to trudge back toward the house.

"No! Leave her be! She'll be okay!" her uncle shouted, but Cherry could neither hear, nor understand as she continued to struggle through the worsening storm and on toward the terrified little dog. Using the porch railing for leverage, she pulled herself up the steps, onto the porch, and up to the open doorway.

Pulling and tugging with as much strength as she could muster, she snapped and latched the screen, pushed the entry door shut and secured the bolt. She flew to the enclosed service porch, the little dog at her heels, and scooped up the litter of newborn pups, placing them securely inside her zippered jacket.

"Come on, Molly! Stay with me," she ordered, as she snatched a comforter from the laundry table next to the dryer, and then ran to the small closet near the center of the house. Later, Uncle Henry would question her about how she knew where to go, what to do, but for now, her only thought was to find someplace safe, and as far away from the storm as she could get.

Draping the comforter over her head and shoulders, she sat cross-legged and leaned against the closet wall. Molly crawled into her lap, as Cherry unzipped her jacket, the puppies tumbling out onto their mother's soft fur. As Molly tucked in her brood, Cherry pulled the comforter snuggly around them and waited.

The house shook, the shutters banged, slamming repeatedly against the windowsills. It sounded like all the shingles were being ripped off the roof by the sheer force of the storm, but still she waited, and waited, for what seemed forever. She thought of Dorothy in "The Wizard of Oz," but that was just a story— this was real.

Small objects dropped from the shelf above, and she pulled the comforter tighter still. She squeezed her eyes shut until they hurt. *Uncle Henry, Sam, where are you? Help me. Help me.* But there was no help forthcoming as the funnel drew closer and closer. She pushed the debris away from the comforter, and shifted just enough to take a quick peek at what had fallen.*Crash.*

Cherry grabbed the back of her head, a knot the size of a hen's egg rapidly forming. Dizziness threatened to overtake her, as she rubbed at the knot. What had hit her? Temporarily blinded by pain, she reached down to check on Molly and the pups. *Okay . . . everything seems . . . okay . . . except for . . . splitting . . . headache.*

Silence.

* * *

She heard a soft whimper, as the doorknob to the closet began to turn. She opened her eyes and stared, blurry-eyed as the door opened and a grinning Sam reached down to take her hand.

"Pop! I found her! Come on Cherry. Need any help up?"

She breathed a sigh of relief. The storm was over, and she was safe. "If you can get Molly and her pups, I think I can get up by myself." Her hand dropped to her lap. Empty. She began to panic. "Where's Molly? Where's the puppies?"

"Uh, puppies? Molly's right here, but what puppies are you talking about?"

"The storm . . . . I rescued Molly, *and* her puppies. They were right here . . . in my lap."

The little sheltie whimpered, jumped into Cherry's lap and began to lick her cheek.

Uncle Henry squatted in front of her and placed his hand against her forehead. "You all right, little one?"

Uncle Henry? Where did he come from?

Her Uncle took her hand, patted it gently, and pulled her to her feet. "Come on, girl. Supper's waitin'."

Cherry stood and shook her head as if to clear it. Molly began dancing around her feet, as she walked unsteadily toward the front door. This was so unreal. She was confused. Puppies, then no puppies. Molly . . . here . . . but what happened to the puppies? The storm. She had to see the damage from the storm, to know if it were really real.

She opened the front door, stepped out and gasped. The only words that came to mind were, "Toto. We're not in Kansas anymore."

2/5/99

GUILTY

(Based on a true story)

MRS. FRANKLIN PERCHED rigidly on the edge of her cluttered desk, glaring angrily at her seventh period class. Tap . . . Tap . . . Tap . . . . She slapped her open palm with the flat edge of her ruler. Tap . . . Tap . . . Tap . . . . No one dared to meet her gaze. Instead, they kept their eyes glued to the graffiti covering their desks. Mrs. Franklin was on the warpath, and no one seemed to know why.

Tap . . . Tap . . . Tap . . . . Harder and harder, she slapped, as her mood grew darker. Suddenly she slammed the ruler onto her desk with such force it snapped in two, leaving shattered, jagged edges.

"No one," she finely spoke. "No one will leave this room until I find out the truth—the entire truth. Do you hear and understand?"

Thirty-two students nodded, but not a word was spoken. No demanded confession was coming forth. Finally, a timid voice ventured to speak. "What truth is that, Ma'am?"

"Don't get funny with me, young man. Take a good look at this blackboard, a real good look."

Every eye flew to the blackboard—the one to the right of Mrs. Franklin's desk.

"Yes, Ma'am," he said, and then asked, "What am I looking *for*, Ma'am?"

"Describe it for me." She folded her arms across her chest and dared him to speak.

"I see a blackboard, Ma'am. A nice, clean blackboard."

"Clean." She raised the pitch of her voice to a near scream. "*Clean!* Can anyone tell me what tonight is?"

A half-dozen voices rang out. "Open House?" they asked hopefully.

"Open House," she acknowledged, sarcasm dripping with each word. "And why was this open house so—"

"Oh, my God!" someone cried from the back of the room. "The chalk mural. It's gone!"

"That's right. Gone! Weeks' worth of painstaking work, gone, vanished, ka-put. *Erased!* And one of *you* did it."

A flood of denials spewed forth, but Mrs. Franklin held firm in her belief. "If you'll recall, I had to leave a few minutes early yesterday. Since you are an honors class, I thought I could trust you to clean up, and lock up, making sure everything was secure. But no. Someone obviously lagged behind and ruined *my* mural."

"Mrs. Franklin," said Sheila, who just happened to be class president. "It wasn't us. I locked up, myself, yesterday, and the mural was still there when we left."

Mrs. Franklin appeared bewildered. "Well, if it wasn't you, then who in the world sabotaged my mural? It was the best thing we've ever done." She looked as if she was ready to burst into tears.

Just then, the classroom door opened, and Mr. Johnson, the head custodian, peered around the corner. "Don't mean to bother you, Mrs. Franklin," he said. "I just wanted to check and see how you liked your room. You bein' our favorite teacher, and all, I told the boys to do an extra good job for you, this bein' open house and all. Hope everything met with your satisfaction."

IN THE BOTTOM OF THE BAG

(Lunch-time chant for elementary grades)

In the bottom of the bag, somewhere, somewhere
in the bottom of the bag, somewhere.
There is something in the bag, somewhere, somewhere
in the bottom of the bag, somewhere.

In the bottom of the bag, somewhere, somewhere
in the bottom of the bag, somewhere.
There's an apple in the bag, somewhere, somewhere
in the bottom of the bag, somewhere.

In the bottom of the bag, somewhere, somewhere
in the bottom of the bag, somewhere.
There's a sandwich in the bag, somewhere, somewhere
in the bottom of the bag, somewhere.

In the bottom of the bag, somewhere, somewhere
in the bottom of the bag, somewhere.
There's a cookie in the bag, somewhere, somewhere
in the bottom of the bag, somewhere.

In the bottom of the bag, somewhere, somewhere
in the bottom of the bag, somewhere.
There's a juice box in the bag, somewhere, somewhere.
in the bottom of the bag, somewhere.

In the bottom of the bag, somewhere, somewhere
in the bottom of the bag, somewhere.
There's a napkin in the bag, somewhere, somewhere
in the bottom of the bag, somewhere.

In the bottom of the bag, somewhere, somewhere
in the bottom of the bag, somewhere.
There's a hand in the bag, searching, reaching
to the bottom of the bag...

LET'S EAT!

KIARA'S BIG DAY

KIARA STARED AT the stranger in the mirror, who was intently staring back at her. She wrinkled her nose and stuck out her tongue. So did the girl in the mirror. She swallowed hard, and snatched a paper towel from the dispenser, wiping imaginary sweat from her brow. Thick black lashes surrounded milk-chocolate-eyes, a few wisps of hair, springing from her hairline, tickling her eyebrows. Her tight black curls had been brushed and pulled and twisted until finally secured with a pony tail clip and tied with a red, white, and blue ribbon to match her dress. She took a deep breath, and leaned slightly over the bathroom counter to get a better look.

"Well, Kiara. I guess it really is you . . . I mean . . . me." But the girl in the mirror was beautiful, not some poor kid from the wrong side of the tracks with patched clothing, one size too big. She was nervous, she was scared, but she was the one who had been chosen. Kiara Green had been chosen to sing "The National Anthem" at the Flag raising ceremony in Charleston Square. Twenty other eleven through thirteen-year-old girls had auditioned for the part, but Kiara was the first black American to have ever been chosen. She was happy, she was proud, but could she really do it?

"Kiara, come on! You're going to be late."

"I'm coming, Mama. Do you think I look all right?"

"You look beautiful, but no one is going to see you if we don't get a move on. Come on, girl. Let's go."

`"Will Daddy be there?"

"I really can't say, but your grandparents will be there, and I'll be there, and . . . everyone will finally see what a wonderful, talented young lady you are." She smiled at her only daughter. "I'm so proud of you." She put an arm around Kiara's shoulders and gave her a quick hug.

"Thank you, Mama." Kiara loved her mother, but it was her father who taught her how to sing, how to stand up for herself, and how to take a chance on life. It was her father who gave her the courage to try out for the coveted solo. For the last two years, Cassandra, the mayor's daughter, had won the part, and had bragged about winning this year too, only . . . she didn't.

Kiara smiled to herself. Daddy had been so proud, but now it didn't look like he was going to be able to make it to her performance after all. She wouldn't cry. She wouldn't. But Mama could tell him all about it later . . . if she would.

As they entered the square, Kiara was quickly escorted to the biggest float in the parade and strapped onto a post to help keep her steady and secure. She was grateful for the restraint, but felt a little claustrophobic, and a bit nauseous. If only Daddy was here, she'd feel much better. She scanned the crowd, waved at her mother and grandparents, but her father was nowhere to be seen. It wasn't his fault, she was sure, but even so she missed him. She was determined to make him proud of her even if he couldn't come to see her perform.

"Hey, you!"

Kiara turned, smiling, searching for the face of the caller. Cassandra. Her smile froze at the look on Cassie's face.

"I just wanted to let you to know you only got the part because you're black and poor and everybody felt sorry for you," Cassandra sneered, before turning her back and stalking off.

Kiara was stunned. Was that the reason she got the part? Did people feel sorry for her?

Don't you listen to no sour grapes, girl. Her father's voice echoed in her mind. *You got what it takes. Do me proud. Daddy loves you, girl. Don't you forget it now.*

Kiara laid her hand against her stomach as the float jerked into motion, slowly following the marching band. *Some* people looked surprised to see *her* standing in the middle of the float, instead of the mayor's daughter, but they smiled and waved just the same. Kiara smiled and waved back, just like she had seen the queen wave in that princess movie last year. It didn't matter what Cassandra said. *She* was the one riding on the float, and *she* was the one who would be singing "The National Anthem" for the ceremony. She stood tall, lifting her head regally, just like Daddy had told her to. She could do this. She would make her father proud.

Out of the corner of her eye, Kiara watched Cassie as she paralleled the float, her fingers at her forehead forming a tiny 'L'. *Loser*, she mouthed, but Kiara flashed a brilliant smile and thought *sour grapes, only sour grapes.*

At last, they entered the square, and Kiara was quickly ushered to a small stage where the city council sat and waited. As the huge new flag was being raised, the mayor rose and handed Kiara a microphone. "Do us proud, girl," she heard, but she wasn't quite certain if she really had heard a voice, or if it had come from her mind. *Do us proud.*

The band began to play and she began to sing: clear, and pure, and beautiful. *This is for you Daddy*, she whispered with her heart, *wherever you are.*

The crowd stood, silent, reverent, as the final notes were sung. One, and then another, and yet another, began to applaud, until the small square swelled for the love of country, the flag, and an eleven-year-old girl who had been chosen. A bouquet of flowers was thrust into her arms, and she turned to thank the giver.

"Daddy," she cried, "you came."

"You done good, girl," was all he could say, with tears in his eyes. "You done good."

"Thank you Daddy," she whispered. And she threw herself into her father's waiting arms.

4/23/99

RAIN

Why does it always have to rain
when I am not in school?
I should be at the park or at
the public swimming pool.

It never, ever seems to rain
when I *can't* go and play.
But when I have some time for fun,
it rains 'most every day.

Now if I had a garden
I suppose it'd be just grand,
to water all my flowers
everyday, like it was planned.

But I don't have a garden,
and it's Saturday to boot.
So here I'm stuck inside my house
just sitting, looking cute.

Disgusting!

I guess I should be happy.
It could be a whole lot worse.
I could be struck by lightning, or
zapped by a mummy's curse.

Shudder . . .

HEY!

The sun has started shining,
and the rain has gone away.
Now things look so much brighter, so . . .
Good bye! I'm out to play.

2/12/99

THE LETTERS

I took my little brother
to the mailbox down the lane,
to mail some special letters,
and see if any came.

We always hope for something,
but nothing ever comes.
We sit and wait forever
just twiddling our thumbs.

It seems like everybody else
gets lots and lots of things -
Such pretty cards and letters,
whatever each day brings.

They place them on the mantle
so everyone can see,
they haven't been forgotten
like little Tim and me.

So I'll take this special letter,
and mail it to myself,
so I can get a letter,
and place it on the shelf.

And won't my little brother
be surprised as he can be,
when he gets a special letter
from his favorite sister, ME!

3/21/02

THE SECRET UNDER THE STAIRS

JOSHUA PETERS WOKE with a start, stretched his long skinny arms, before lacing his fingers behind his head, and grinned. This was going to be a great day. It wasn't just because it was Thanksgiving, and the smells wafting upstairs were sending shivers of anticipation to each of his senses, and it wasn't just because all the aunts, uncles and cousins—ah, yes, the cousins—could be here at any moment, and it wasn't because this was also his birthday—well, maybe just a tad.

No. Today was Josh's big day. Today he was ten, and that meant no more sitting at the 'baby' table. Today he graduates to the 'big kids' table. All of his life he had longed to sit with the big kids. Only there could he find adventure, prestige, and find out what girls do when boys aren't around. Yes, today was his lucky day. He hummed in his off-key manner as he dressed and prepared for the adventures of the day.

Promptly at two o'clock in the afternoon, the family was seated, and Uncle James was delivering the blessing. Joshua sat smugly at his end of the table, and waited to be noticed. At last the food was blessed, and forty-two starving bodies were chowing down.

"Hey, Dweeb. What are you doing here? *This* is the *men's* table. Go back to the *baby* table where you belong."

Joshua crossed his arms, stuck out his chin, and smiled at his 14 year-old brother, Steven. "I *am* where I belong," he said.

"Not in this lifetime, Pipsqueak."

"Oh yeah? That's not what Mother said."

"Mother is a girl. How do you expect her to know anything about men?"

"Well, I—"

"Boys? I hope I don't hear any bickering out there. Remember, this is a day to be thankful for all the good Lord has given us. I hope I don't have to come out there and *remind* you."

"No, Mother. We're just having a little fun."

"Well, that's good. And don't pick on your brother. It's his birthday, you know."

"Heeey, that's right, little bro'." With a glint in his eye, Steven crouched next to Joshua and said. "Don't worry, Josh. *We'll* see that your birthday is *prop*-erly celebrated."

"Don't bother. I'd rather celebrate by myself."

"Oh, really? Would you like to excuse yourself, and go back to where you belong?"

"I *am* where I belong."

"Suit yourself." Steven moved back to the head of the table, and the six older cousins resumed their conversation.

Joshua's scowl deepened as he slid lower into his captain's chair. *Hmmm,* he thought. *This is no fun.* He glanced around the room, and then suddenly began to brighten. "Hey," he said, but no one paid any attention to him. He sat straighter in his chair, and again said, "Hey!" this time just a bit louder.

"What?" Six pairs of eyes were now on him.

"I know a secret," he said.

"What can a baby like you know that we don't already know?" asked Matthew the Terrible—he was Steven's age, but twice as obnoxious.

"I know what's in the cupboard under the stairs."

"You can't," said Steven. "No way. Mother's kept that door padlocked ever since I can remember."

"Yes I can, and I'm not telling!"

The boys begged and pleaded for several minutes, but Joshua stubbornly refused to give in.

"Back off, boys," said Steven. "I'll get him to talk."

"Wanna bet? I'm not telling *you* anything."

"You don't know what I have to bargain with, yet, pea-brain, I mean favorite brother of mine."

"Nothing *you* have would ever interest me."

"Nothing? Well, take a look at this." He pulled a clear glass bobble, flattened on one side, out of his pocket and laid it on the table, just out of reach.

"*That's* your bargain? It's nothin' but a dumb piece of glass."

"Not so, me hearty." Steven caressed the stone as if it had great value. "You remember Mr. Bloomfield, down at Miller's Boarding House?" Joshua nodded. "Well, he made me work one whole summer for it. Wouldn't give it up 'till school started. Wanta know why?" Joshua nodded again and gulped. "It seems, nice old Mr. Bloomfield's great-great grandfather was a pirate, and stole it fair and square from some merchant ship carrying a king's ransom in jewels. Belonged to some Maharajah in India, I think he said."

"India? Pirate, you say? Let me see it."

"No can do. Not unless we have a legal trade. You tell, I *may* sell—information that is."

"Sorry, my lips are sealed. I'd need more information to—"

"*You're* asking *me* for more info?"

Joshua nodded, knowing he had the upper hand, at least for the time being.

"You're really askin' for it, kid."

"Hey, Steve," Matthew cut in. "Do you want to know what your mom's got hidden or not?"

"All right, already." He glared at Joshua. "But *you* better put out afterwards. What makes this rock special? Well, I'll tell you. As I already said, it belonged to a Maharajah who lived in India. He was very, very rich, and had lots of treasure, but this was his very favorite piece. You see, he not only had lots of money, but lots of wives too—ten in all, according to Mr. Bloomfield. Anyway, this stone was called a dancing stone, and was specially made to be glued into a belly dancer's . . . well, stomach. All ten of the rajah's wives were super dancers, and were treated better than most women of the time.

"Now, the rajah loved to watch them dance, but only one at a time. So every so often, he would send for one of his wives to dance for him. If she pleased him, she was allowed to keep the stone, for a while, and was treated with great respect, with all the privileges of the number one wife. As long as she had the stone, she knew everything was okay, but as soon as the rajah fancied another, the stone was taken back, given to the next wife, and the first returned to the harem, or whatever they called them in India."

"That doesn't sound so bad," said Joshua.

"Not if the rajah liked their dancing," said Steven. "But, if he didn't—" He leaned so close to his brother, his breath left wisps of foggy patterns on his glasses.

"What?" A weird tingle tickled the back of Josh's neck.

"He took the stone back, and cut off their heads."

Joshua swallowed hard, but tried his best not to flinch or show signs of throwing up. Straining to gain back some composure, he asked, "So? How did the rock get on the ship?"

"After his last wife *disappeared*, he decided to travel the world and search for some better ones. Took the stone with him. After all, what's a dancer without a stone? When the pirates took the stone, he didn't have anything to bargain with anymore. So he went home. Rumor was he went crazy after that. Day after day, he moaned about that stone. And *I've* got it. I'm waiting for my own dancing girls." He rolled his eyes, and made a rude gesture.

The cousins howled with laughter as Joshua said, "You're disgusting. Did you know that?"

"Disgusting are we?" Joshua's words seemed to have a disquieting effect on the boys as Steven grabbed a chair, and plopped down next to his brother. "So, you think we're disgusting, do you? Okay. Fun and games are over. I did my part, now you do yours."

The only thing that kept Joshua from falling onto the floor was the heavy arm of the chair, digging deeply into his shoulder blade. Frantically, his mind raced, trying to think of anything to appease his brother and his cousins. *I don't know, I don't know*, he thought, near tears.

"Well? Spill yer guts, me bucko, before I spill them for ya."

"You're nuts! You've been watching too many old movies. I'm going to tell Mom."

"Forget Mom. This is just between us *men*. Now tell!"

Joshua gulped once more, straightened his shoulders, and stared eye to eye with his brother. "Sorry, my lips are sealed. Besides, Mother would kill me."

"What makes you think you're safe here?" The boys snickered. "Man yer weapons, men."

One slightly worn rubber band emerged from someone's pocket, and was aimed straight at Joshua's trembling heart.

"Ah, forget it, Steve," said Matthew. "He doesn't know anything. If he did, he would have told already. Let's send him back to the baby table, where he belongs."

The cousins picked up the chair, with Josh tightly gripping the arms, and started toward the door.

"Boys? What are you up to?"

Hearing their aunt's voice, the boys quickly returned the chair to its proper place, and sat at their own. This time Matthew crouched in front of Joshua, a sneer upon his face. "Well, little man," he said. "If you really *do* know the secret, tell us how *you* found out, and what's in there."

"Well, I—"

"Hurry it up. We're losing our patience."

"Um-m-m. We-ell. There's a crack in one of the stairs where you can see in."

"That's it? Everybody knows that. The problem is, it's just too dark to see anything, even if you tried 24/7. So how could *you* see in the dark—X-ray vision, or what?"

Joshua began to think he just might live after all and began to explain, "I had to get up one night to—you know, when I saw Mother sneaking downstairs, so I followed her. She went into the room and turned on the light. She had something in her hand when she went in and nothing when she came out. I was laying on the stairs, peeking through the crack, so I saw everything."

"Like what?"

"Oh. Just things." It was true he had followed his mother, and he had peeked through the crack, but with his mother blocking the view, he really couldn't see much of anything. "Don't ask me anymore," he said. "My life could be in danger."

The boys looked with new respect at Joshua. Maybe, for a kid, he was all right.

"Hey, look," someone whispered. "Your Mom's about to open the room. She's got the key out. She's sticking it in the padlock. It's turning. It's off. She's opening the door. She's going in. She's coming out. *What* is that?"

Mrs. Peters handed her packages to Steven, and locked the door. Mr. Peters walked through the kitchen door, ten candles blazing on a three-layer chocolate marble fudge cake.

"HAPPY BIRTHDAY!"

Joshua was stunned as his father set the cake on the table before him, and Steven set the stack of presents next to it. He pointed his right index finger at Joshua and said, "Gotcha.

33

Welcome to the *men's* table," as he and the cousins pounded the birthday boy on his back.

Joshua fingered the stone Steven had slipped him, and knew for a fact he had been scammed. But he didn't mind in the least, for it was on this, his tenth birthday, that he had at last become a man. But, even better than that, he had finally discovered the secret of what was hidden underneath the stairs—or had he?

2/13/11

TWICE-BAKED BEANS

N ICKY PULLED HER apron over her head and tied it carefully behind her back. This was her birthday, and the
one thing she liked better than anything else in the
whole world was Grandma Nell's super-delicious baked-beans.
Grandma Nell made the best baked-beans ever, and on this
birthday Nicky got to help make them.

"What do I do now, Grandma?" she asked.

"Well," said Grandma. "First we need to gather all of the ingredients. Let's see. We need dry mustard, molasses – the dark kind,
brown sugar, garlic, bacon, salt pork, those chopped onions and
. . . don't forget the secret ingredients." She smiled as Nicky ran
to the cupboard and grabbed the jar labeled 'S.I.'. She stirred the
beans one last time and set them aside.

Almost before she knew it, the beans were in the oven, and
Nicky was licking her lips in anticipation. She rubbed at her
tummy, on the right side, and moaned, just a little.

"Nicky?" Grandma asked. "Are you okay?"

"It's just a little pain, Grandma. It'll go away."

"Show me where." She touched the spot, and Nicky jumped,
crying out in pain. "When did this start, Nicky?"

"This morning." She leaned to one side, pressing on the spot.

"Why didn't you tell me, dear?" Grandma Nell looked worried. *Appendicitis?*

"I wanted . . . to help with the beans." She began to cry.

"The beans can wait. We need to take you to the doctor."

* * *

Three days later Mama picked Nicky up from the hospital and carefully tucked her into the back seat of their van. "Why so glum, Nicky? We're going home. Don't you want to go home?"

"I guess so," she sighed. But she couldn't stop thinking about her birthday, baked beans, and that she had missed them both.

Mama pulled into the driveway and helped Nicky into the house. As she walked through the door, the smell of baked beans made her heart jump.

"Beans?"

Her mother nodded and smiled. Grandma Nell poked her head around the kitchen door and motioned for Nicky to come into the kitchen.

Streamers were everywhere. Balloons hung from the ceiling. A huge "Happy Birthday" sign covered one whole wall, and a pink and white birthday cake with seven candles sat in the middle of the table. She hadn't missed her birthday after all.

Nicky's eyes grew big and her jaw dropped as Grandma set the pot of beans on a hot pad right next to the cake. "We saved them for you," Grandma Nell smiled. "Twice-baked beans." She put some in a bowl and set it in front of Nicky.

Nicky grabbed her spoon and dipped it into the beans. She blew on them and took a bite. *Yummm.* She grinned. "Grandma. You make the best 'twice-baked beans' ever."

And she did.

WHO FILCHED THE PIE

Mrs. Potts baked a pie.

Mrs. Potts baked a plum pie.

Mrs. Potts baked a purple plum pie.

Mrs. Potts baked a purple plum pie for Mr. Potts.

Mrs. Potts placed the purple plum pie on the kitchen counter to cool.

When the pie was cool, Mrs. Potts went into the kitchen to store the pie for supper, but . . . the pie was gone.

Gone! Oh my! Who filched the pie?

"But then again," she tapped her head, "I've had a busy day. Perhaps in my forgetfulness I put the pie away."

Mrs. Potts searched high.

Mrs. Potts searched low.

She checked every cupboard above and below.

But the pie was not there.

She peeked in the oven.

She checked the fridge twice.

She glanced in the freezer, all covered with ice.

But the pie was not there.

She searched through the pantry. She checked every shelf. But Mr. Potts' purple plum pie was nowhere to be found. Mrs. Potts was worried. What could she do?

Mr. Potts must have his pie, but there wasn't time to make another. Gone. Oh my.

"WHO FILCHED THE PIE?!"

"Not I," said Jenny Potts as she entered the kitchen, her lips shining with purple goo.

"Not you, indeed," scolded Mrs. Potts. "I see your lips say otherwise."

"On no," said Jenny. "It's my new purple lipstick." She held it out for her mother to see.

"Hmmm," said Mrs. Potts. "Then who?"

"Hmmm," said Jenny. "I wonder who? Was it you?" she asked as Jimmy Potts walked into the kitchen, purple from his nose to his chin.

"Not I," said Jimmy, licking his grape-flavored all-day sucker.

"Then who," puzzled Mrs. Potts? "I certainly didn't eat it." She tapped her head as she tapped her foot. "Now who—"

"Now who," said Jenny?

"Now who," echoed Jimmy? "Was it you," he asked, as little Jamie Potts entered the kitchen? "Did you filch the pie?"

"Not I," said Jamie, as she took a big sloppy bite of her peanut butter and grape jelly sandwich.

"Then who," said Mrs. Potts?

"Then who," said Jenny?

"Then who," echoed Jimmy?

"Who knows," shrugged Jamie?

Just then Shaggy Filbert stuck his purple muzzle through the kitchen doorway, but when he saw Mrs. Potts and the children he backed up and quietly disappeared.

"Hmmm," said Mrs. Potts as she and the children quickly followed the shaggy pup through the hall and into the den. And what do you think they found?

There, sitting in his favorite chair, sat Mr. Potts and the baby, covered with Mrs. Potts freshly baked purple plum pie.

"Hmmm," said Mrs. Potts, her hands on her hips.

"Hmmm," said Jenny.

"Hmmm," echoed Jimmy.

"Where's mine," grumbled Jamie?

"Yummm," smiled Mr. Potts, as he ate the very last bite.

2/9/11

WHOSE MOUSE IS THIS?

"**L**OL-LIE!"

Uh-oh. Lollie glanced toward the empty cage and sighed. Not again. She threw back her covers, just as her parents, and her sometimes-cool older brother, Jason, walked into her bedroom.

Her father marched up to her holding a small white mouse by the tail, and said, "Whose mouse is this?"

"Uh . . . mine?"

"And where should he be?"

"He was in his cage last night. I swear! I don't know how he keeps getting out."

"Well, little girl, you had best do something about it, and quick. Do you want to know where I found him this time?"

Lollie wasn't certain whether she wanted to know or not, but she kept quiet and listened anyway.

"Sleeping . . . on my best pipe." He dropped the little mouse into her open palm. "He *gnawed* on the bowl. I do *not* want it to happen again."

"Yeah," said Jason. "And if he chews up another one of my socks, he's a rat-burger."

40

"But . . . ." She put the mouse back in his cage. She didn't know how he was always escaping, but she knew if he did it again, he would be toast. A large black cat crept in and leaped onto the dresser, his eyes half-closed, staring intently at the little mouse, licking his chops. Lollie could almost see drool dripping.

"Down, Midnight! Go Away!"

Midnight, the family cat, was Lollie's greatest fear. If Monty was to get out when Midnight was about, the little mouse wouldn't have a chance. Lollie had done everything she could think of to keep him safe. Once, she had even used her best ribbon to tie the cage-door closed, but the next morning Monty was gone, and the ribbon was inside his cage. He wasn't even safe in his hamster-ball. That cat loved to attack poor Monty's ball, chasing and batting it around the room. Something had to be done.

That night, Lollie tried to stay awake and catch the little escape-artist in action. But she soon fell fast asleep. Just before dawn she was awakened by a tiny squeak. Lollie quickly switched on her flashlight, and pointed it at the cage. There was Midnight, holding the cage door open with one paw. But . . . where was Monty?

Two shiny black eyes, in a ball of white fur, peered at her from between Midnight's ears, as the cat slowly let the door fall.

"Midnight! *You've* been letting Monty out? Bad cat!"

Lollie suddenly realized that Midnight didn't want to *eat* Monty. He just wanted a friend. But just in case—

Later that day:

Lollie walked through her bedroom door with two bags in her hand. One she took and emptied into Monty's cage. "There," she said. "Now you have someone your own size to play with." The little mice sniffed noses, as she slipped the new metal clip into place and snapped it shut. Now there was no way they could get out.

Midnight stared mournfully at the little mice. "Don't worry. I've got one for you too." She reached into the second bag and pulled out Midnight's surprise. She wound the key and set the toy mouse on the ground. The chase was on.

.

CHRISTMAS/HOLIDAY

SPRING 2008

A CHRISTMAS POEM

Christmas time is coming.
The best time of the year,
when all the little children wait
for Santa to appear.

They hope to catch a glimpse of him
when down the flue he comes.
They know that Santa's pack is full
with toys, c d's and drums.

But Santa knows just what to do.
He waits till they're asleep.
He doesn't want to spoil the fun.
He works without a peep.

And so on Christmas morning
when all the children rise,
they'll find that Santa's been there.
Oh, my! What a surprise!

2/7/02

JEREMIAH'S BAD DAY

J EREMIAH WEATHERSLY STOOD, with his right elbow in his left paw, his chin in his right paw and his right index finger tap, tap, tapping upon the side of his fuzzy old head. A deep scowl reached from his chin to the tips of his long, slender ears, which twitched in time with the tap, tap, tapping on his head. Jeremiah Weathersly had a problem.

As head rabbit of Egg-drop-way station, he was responsible for picking up all eggs meant for Easter, and seeing that they were well boiled, painted, decorated and sent on their way to the packing and transportation department. But they were already three hours late.

"Oh, me, oh, my," he groaned, worry lines creasing his forehead. For the umpteenth time, he checked his grandfather's old pocket watch for the correct time: eleven o'clock and no train. And no train meant no eggs. And no eggs meant nothing to boil, paint, and decorate for the children's Easter baskets.

"It's those hens, I'll warrant," he grumbled. "Laziest bunch we ever had. Don't they realize we have a quota to fill? Maybe it's not the hens. Maybe the train flew off the track. Oh dear, oh dear. What to do? What to do? No eggs, no baskets. What *are* we going to do? Tsk, tsk, tsk. Not a word. Narry a word. What to do?"

He began pacing back and forth, forth and back, following the same slight groove in the old pine platform his father, and his father before him had fashioned. *I'm not as young as I used to be*, he thought.

My nerves, my poor nerves. Oh, what to do, what to do. "I'm getting far too old for this," he groaned, his shoulders bent, his pace slowing to barely a crawl. *Oh, worry, worry, worry.*

"Relax, ol' buddy, ol' pal. All is not lost."

Jeremiah stared at his tall, lanky nephew, Jack. "What are YOU doing here, you scoundrel? You've never done an honest day's work in your life. Just have to pester the life out of me as usual, I suppose."

"Uncle Jeremiah, you wound me. I just came to tell you to go home. Train's not comin'."

"Nonsense! Every Wednesday before Easter, for longer than I can remember, the train has arrived, never late. Never, never," he sighed.

"Well that's it, then," Jack smiled broadly.

"What's it?"

"Why, today is Tuesday." He put his arm around Jeremiah's shoulders and jauntily walked him home. After all, tomorrow was going to be a busy, busy day.

2/18/99

MY CHRISTMAS WISH

Christmas time is coming,
and I've been very good.
I've mowed the lawn, and raked the leaves
just like I knew I should.

I've shoveled snow, and helped my dad
to trim the yuletide log.
I helped my sister clean her room.
I even fed the dog.

I did the very best I could.
My little sis did too . . .
in hopes our folks would notice
with Christmas coming due.

I asked my father for a car.
He bought a ten-speed bike.
My sister begged, "A pony please."
She only got a trike.

So then we asked old Santa Claus.
He said, "All in good time."
I sure do hope that he comes through
before I'm ninety-nine.

1/16/02

THE WISH

I T'S VERY STRANGE – the light of day. Oh, I've seen it many times, but each time the wonder seems all the more. I lay in my box, wrapped in many layers of tissue paper, sleeping, until just the right moment to wake and see the world anew.

I don't really serve a useful purpose. I'm not beautiful, and no one really pays any attention to me. But that's all right. What good is a candle anyway, especially one who has never been lit? I don't know how old I am, but I'm sure I must be of considerable age. I've seen three generations of children grow up in this house, including the present ones of course. I've been passed from hand to hand, but never touched by children. "It might break," I hear, and I wonder what that might feel like – to break. But I will never know, I suppose.

I was fashioned many years ago by childish hands. I was her first, and last. She used to hold me, caress me, but then she was gone, and I was put into the box. I missed her so. I often wonder why she went away and did not take me with her. But no one ever tells a candle anything. So I sleep - fifty weeks out of the year.

My awakening begins precisely at 8:00 in the morning on each December 19th. Every year it's the same. I am carefully unwrapped and placed on the mantle for everyone to see. But no one ever looks my way. But that's all right. From where I stand, I can see everything. It's a grand sight: the colors, the smells, the beauty of Christmas. It's a good life I have, but lonely.

I spend my days dreaming of what it might be like to be something different. Perhaps I could be a tree, heavy with delicate ornaments, brilliant with twinkling dots of lights, shimmering with strands of silver. Ah. How special I would feel to be adorned so. Or perhaps I could do well as a Christmas train. Around and around the track I would go – clickedy-clack, clickedy-clack, making the dear children happy. Ah, yes. Such would be the life.

I listen to them talk, sometimes – the tree and the train. It's sad, really, for such a happy time. "My branches become heavier each year," complains the tree. "It's getting to where I can hardly lift them anymore." What I would give to feel the weight of those branches.

"Well," interrupted the little engine. "You should try being a train. Around and around in circles, day after day with no place to go - just around and around and around. My wheels are beginning to wear thin. It becomes harder each year to even stay on the track. What a miserable life I lead."

"You should talk," cried the caboose. "My paint is peeling from years of sticky, little fingers. Disgusting, I say."

And I stand there, silently, wishing I could feel sticky little fingers caressing me. But such is not to be. For I am out of reach, high upon the mantle where I stand and keep vigil until I am placed back in my box. I wish I could stay up here forever. I'd love to see the spring. I hear it's lovely.

"Don't feel badly." A gentle voice slips between my dreams. "Rejoice while you can." It's the angel of the crèche. She is beautiful. She sits on a small platform overlooking the Holy child, a bright star held gently in her hands, illuminating the manger. And I think how wonderful it would be to light the way for the shepherds, the wise men, to lead them to the babe. I think I would like that best.

As I am dreaming these lovely dreams, I watch as our angel of the crèche slowly turns. I wonder why, but she speaks not a word until her light reflects from the silver strands of the tree, and the mottled chrome of the little engine. "Why do you grumble and complain so?" she asks. "Without the children there would be no need for you. You should be ashamed of yourselves. 'Tis the birthday of the Holy One, the Blessed Child. Rejoice. Be happy to be of service, and worship the Holy Child as best you can, for without Him, you might not have been."

But the tree and the train are too wrapped up in self-pity to listen; though they know in their hearts she speaks the truth. She turns sadly, and resumes her post, once again lighting the way to the Babe.

* * *

It's Christmas Eve and I am content. The family is gathered all around. Tiny hands, sticky from unwrapped sweets, are caressing the little caboose and pushing the tired engine around the track. There are no complaints now. Music and laughter fill the air. It's Christmas Eve and all is well.

But all is not well. A wee child is sobbing. "It's all right, my darling," croons his mother. "Daddy will mend her in the morning."

I am filled with sorrow. The china angel lies in pieces on the floor, sticky fingerprints upon her wings. The manger lies in darkness and I weep. What to do? What to do?

But what is happening? I am being lifted from my post upon the mantle. It's not yet time. "Please. Don't put me back in the box," I try to say. "I am not ready." But no one hears. I close my eyes and wait. I can't bear to go back to sleep so soon. And then I feel . . . feel . . . what? A warmth—a glow about me. I feel suddenly alive.

"She would want it this way," I hear.

I slowly open my eyes. The shadow of a lop-sided angel rests upon the crèche, and the manger is illuminated once again. My heart soars as I glance around me. I see myself for the first time in the eyes of those who surround me, and I think to myself, "At last I have a purpose."

And then, in quiet wonder, I hear a child's voice sweetly say, "This is the most beautiful angel of all."

And I am happy.

DRAMATIC

2/2/99

COMING OF AGE

"GEORGIA . . . Georgia! Please hurry with that table. Uncle Mike and Aunt Martha could be here at any moment. I told them dinner would be ready by seven o'clock, and it's already six-thirty past now.

"Sure, Mom." Georgia absently studied the nearly completed place settings, fidgeting with napkins and silverware. "Mom? Can I ask you a question?"

"Hmmm . . . I suppose it depends on just how *personal* it is," her mother replied.

"Mom!"

"Oh, all right, go ahead. But please work a little faster. We'll never make it at this rate."

"*Mom!*"

"All right, already, ask away."

"Uh . . . ." Georgia hesitated, then blurted. "Did you and Dad ever . . . uh . . . you know, before you got married."

"Georgia," Mrs. Blackwell gasped. "That's really none of your business."

"I guess that means yes, huh."

"It means nothing of the kind. And if you *must* know, your father had barely gotten around to kissing me by the time we got married."

"Oh . . . So I guess your wedding night was quite a revelation."

Mrs. Blackwell stopped what she was doing, stared for a moment at her only daughter and asked, "Okay, Georgia. What's this all about? You've never been this interested in my love life before. Is something bothering you, or are you just making conversation?"

"Well," Georgia began. "I was just thinking about Uncle Mike and Aunt Martha. Here it is, their first anniversary, and they're spending it with us. Why do you suppose that is, Mom?"

"I suppose it's because your dad and I stood up for them at their wedding, and they'd just like to include us at this special time. And then of course, there's baby Sean." Mrs. Blackwell smiled wistfully.

"That's the other thing, Mom. Sean is four and a half months old, and four and a half from twelve equals . . . Well, they had only been married seven and a half months when Sean was born. Does that seem right to you? Aunt Martha had to have been pregnant when they got married, didn't she?"

"Georgia! How can you say such a thing? Of course she wasn't pregnant. I would have known if she was. We've always been best friends as well as sisters. We always told each other everything. Well . . . almost everything," Mrs. Blackwell said thoughtfully, and then added with determination, "Sean was *definitely* premature."

"But he was almost eight pounds. If he was a premie, you'd think he'd be much smaller."

"Well . . . look at Uncle Mike—six feet, five inches, and 250 pounds. That makes for big babies. There's a history of big babies in his family, you know. I wouldn't worry about it, if I were you. And besides, if Aunt Martha says she was a virgin on her wedding day, then she was. End of conversation." Mrs. Blackwell studied her daughter for a moment, then felt compelled to ask, "Um . . . I know we've not talked much about this before, but . . . uh . . . you haven't . . . uh . . . you know, have you?"

"No, Mom. I think I'm the only kid of my age in the universe that hasn't." Georgia dropped heavily into the nearest chair and sighed. "I know all but two of my friends have, and I'm not really sure those two haven't. I feel almost like an outcast."

"Georgia, dear, you're only fifteen. And I would be extremely surprised if even half of your friends were active. Peer pressure often makes people say things that aren't true, just because they don't want to be the *only* one who hasn't. Now, don't you worry about it. Oh my, look at the time. You, young lady, better high-tail it up those stairs and change. You've got five minutes. Now scat. And Georgia . . . feel free to ask me anything personal any time you feel the need."

Georgia grinned, jumped to her feet, and sprinted up the stairs. "Okay, Mom. I'm holding you to it." She slammed her bedroom door and quickly jerked off her T-shirt and jeans. Kicking her discarded clothing into her closet, she grabbed her favorite white pearl sweater, and red velour skirt, threw them on, brushed and tied her hair back with a matching red ribbon, then carefully examined herself in her full-length mirror. *Better pull this skirt down just a little*, she thought. *Mom will have a cow.* Georgia jumped at the sound of the doorbell.

"Georgia, dear. Hurry down. They're here."

As Georgia headed toward her bedroom doorway, she noticed the closet door still open. As she went to shut it, her eyes gravitated to a small pink package, which had fallen out of her jeans pocket. Gingerly she picked up the still unopened compact, stared at it thoughtfully, for just a moment, slipped it into an old, used manila envelope, and tossed it into the trash. A sense of relief washed over her as she thought to herself, *I guess I won't be needing these after all.* Then she ran down to dinner.

SPRING 2002

FOG

Shadowed figures immersed in uncertainty.
Hidden faces lurking in wisps of gray . . . of silver blue.
Dimly lit, grasping for light, yet-
reveling in the moisture of the air.

Trapped in solitude -
awaiting the lifting, the rising of the mist,
the settling of the droplets, till light returns
to flood the valley with remembrances and life.

MEMORIES

Amber flames lick at the darkness
Shadows drifting here and yon
Memories of past time pleasures
passing, fleeting, nearly gone.

Thoughts of childhood weave their tendrils
Grasping, clinging to my mind
Dragons, fairies, leaping, turning,
leave reality behind.

SECRETS

SILVIA NERVOUSLY TWISTED the antique solitaire around and around the ring finger on her right hand, before reaching up to cradle the tiny gold band swaying gently from the thin gold chain dangling between her breasts. She half-smiled as her thoughts jumped to her husband of six months, but tears filled her eyes at the secrets they held. No one knew about the wedding. No one had been invited to attend. No one would have come if they had been invited.

The Air Force knew, of course. They had to. Her allotment checks came every month, regular as clockwork, but she hadn't spent a penny. Every dime rested securely in the bank gaining what meager interest it could until he came home . . . or the baby arrived . . . whichever came first.

She was an artist, and a good one at that. The few paintings she had sold had allowed her to live comfortably without being forced to use up her precious savings. Unfortunately, she had had to change mediums as the oils made her too ill to paint. The new medium felt strange, but it was either acrylics or give up the only livelihood she knew. But what did it matter now?

Her thoughts rushed back to the day he was deployed; the day she told him of his impending fatherhood. His joy was mixed with concern—for her, for the baby, for the secrets that must be kept. Their marriage had been forbidden, though both were well of age. His parents thought she was unworthy—middle class trash—while hers . . . well, snobbery left a distasteful stench in their mouths they could not stomach, much less accept. 'You can do better,' both families decried. So the secrets began.

The letter came yesterday— We regret to inform you . . . missing in action . . . . She had walked for hours . . . cried for hours. Her life . . . her love . . . missing. *What to do*, her mind screamed. Would the Air Force let his parents know, or would they expect her to relay the message. She shuddered, waves of nausea rolling over her. They would wonder why *she* should have been informed and not they, his parents.

Secrets . . . terrible burdens. They *should* know. But if she went to them, there would be questions, denials, accusations. Her hand slipped to her abdomen. The baby! Would they be able to tell? Would they try to take him from her . . . to raise as their own. No! They must never know. This was *her* child . . . hers and Victor's. She couldn't . . . wouldn't take the chance. But—

* * *

She had felt the first flutterings of life this morning, and was filled with a mixture of profound joy, and overwhelming grief— joy for the new life cradled within her, and grief for a child who may never know his father. She walked. She ran. She cried.

She took the path through the park—the one hugging the lake; the one where she and Victor had spent so many happy hours together strolling arm in arm, too much in love to notice elderly couples remembering . . . remembering. She stopped, too spent to go on, and dropping heavily onto the wrought-iron park bench, buried her head in her lap, her arms swinging limply by her sides. She should go home.

There were decisions to be made, decisions to be made by her alone: decisions which could change the lives of a grieving mother and an unborn child. Decisions . . . . Secrets . . . . Her parents . . . . His . . . . Home . . . .

* * *

It was Friday. Three days had passed since the letter arrived—three days of tossing and turning . . . of pacing and deliberation. She had made her decision. In spite of her fears, his parents must be told. The baby she would keep a secret as long as she could, but his parents had the right to know, had the right to grieve, if grief there must be. Besides, the letter hadn't said he was dead, just missing. He could be anywhere . . . anywhere. She dismissed the niggling at the back of her brain, the persistent pounding that almost every missing service man was either never found, or turned up in a makeshift morgue somewhere.

Almost. That's a big word, almost, and she was determined to believe the best until if and when the unthinkable raised its ugly head and struck. With her head held high, she grabbed her bag, and with umbrella in hand slipped out of her apartment and onto the rain soaked sidewalk. Miserable weather. A bad omen? No, she decided. Just miserable weather . . . .

Droplets of rain caressed her cheeks as silent tears began to trickle slowly from her chin, joining the puddles already forming on the ground. She raised her face toward the heavens, her tears mingling with Heaven's own, and began to sob.

* * *

By the time she reached the mansion she was drenched, but still she stood, her finger poised to push the bell. "Forgive me, Victor," she whispered. Secrets must be told—but not all. She took a deep breath and pushed the button.

"Yeeees?" The butler stood straight and tall, much taller than she remembered him. "Well? What is it? If you are soliciting, we don't want any. If it's anything else, perhaps I can be of service, perhaps not." The Butler's polished British accent would have caused her to smile on any other day, on any other occasion, but this was not one of those occasions.

"Frederick, it's me. Are they home? It's important." She held her purse tightly against her chest, the devastating letter hidden safely in the bottom of her bag.

"Miss Silvia? Is it you? Do come in. It's delightful to see you again. It's been too long. You look positively radiant." He ushered her into the foyer before pausing to add, "Please forgive me. This is really not a good time. The Madame is in, how shall I say it, a frightful mood. She received dastardly news today and everyone is well . . . you know. Miss Silvia, are you all right? You look a bit pale."

"So they know," she murmured, barely above a whisper.

"Know, Miss? Know what, Miss?"

"About the letter—"

"Letter? What letter, Miss? To what are you referring?"

Silvia was confused. "I thought— What news came today? Why was Mrs. Brookhurst so upset?"

"It was terrible, just terrible. You would have thought her world had come to an end. My-oh-my."

Her world. *Victor was her world, as Victor was . . .* **is** *mine. What could be more important than Victor?* "Frederick! Please."

"Ah, yes. You are, of course, familiar with the annual charity ball—the Garden Party Ball. The height of the season. *Her* ball . . . *her* garden. Washed out with this despicable rain. Once a year it's madam's time to shine, and poof, destruction. She is ruined, ruined." He paused, staring at Silvia with guarded concern, mixed with curiosity. "To what were *you* referring, Miss Silvia."

"I need to see them, Frederick . . . both of them."

"Oh dear, Miss. Do you think that's wise . . . under the circumstances?"

Under the circumstances . . . . "Yes, Frederick. It can't be helped. If there was any other way . . . . But there isn't. I need to see them now." *Before my courage runs out, and I run.*

Her boldness surprised them both, but the old Butler knew better than to argue. Perhaps her presence would do Madam good. Anything to stop the whining, the moaning, the—

"Frederick! What is that woman doing here? Have I not repeatedly told you she is not welcome here?"

"Yes, Madam, but she assured me it was of vital importance that she see you today." Frederick turned, eyes twinkling as he smiled briefly at Silvia, and then turned his attention back to his employers.

"Since when have *you* been given permission to make decisions as to—"

"Monica, pipe down! I'm sure Silvia would not have braved the storm, either of them," her husband muttered, "if it was not important. Good morning, my dear. What is it you needed to talk to us about? We're all ears."

"Well," Mrs. Brookhurst bristled. "I never!"

Mr. Brookhurst ignored his wife as he escorted Silvia into the drawing room. "Coming, Monica?"

Silvia followed obediently but refused to sit down. She wanted to get this over with as soon as possible and then run back to her apartment. She was exhausted and needed sleep. She wasn't sure what to think of her father-in-law. She had never before seen him take control of a situation like that, and she wasn't sure how to react. So she simply reached into her purse, retrieved the letter and with shaking hands, laid it on his open palm.

Mr. Brookhurst quietly read the letter before handing it over to his wife.

"What is *this*?" she demanded. "I don't understand. There has got to be a mistake. Why is the Air Force sending *you*, a practical stranger, private information? You stole it, didn't you? Out of our mailbox. That's a federal offence, you know. We could have you arrested. Frederick, call the police."

"Ignore my wife, Frederick. Silvia, you need to sit down. You don't look well. Frederick, get the younger Mrs. Brookhurst a glass of water, will you?"

Silvia did feel a bit faint and allowed her father-in-law to lead her to the antique velvet sofa. A gentle hand, she was not accustomed to. Did he refer to her as the *younger* Mrs. Brookhurst? How could he know?

It was all supposed to be a secret. Does he know about the baby, or does he even suspect? No, he can't. Waves of dizziness were threatening to overcome her as she fought to gain control. Her father-in-law reached out and took her hand, gently patting her fears away.

"I agree with Monica, my dear. There has obviously been a mistake made somewhere. I would know. We have an unbreakable connection, he and I. I'll do everything in my power, use every source at my disposal to find him. So don't you worry your pretty little head, okay?"

"But—" Silvia didn't know what to think, what to do. Never had she been treated this kindly by a Brookhurst, except for Victor, of course. He seemed genuine, but could this be a trick? She wanted to trust him, but should she?

"No buts. We *will* find him and bring him home, one way or the other."

Or the other. She didn't even want to think about 'the other.'

"Trust me?"

Silvia hesitated only briefly before answering. "Yes, I do." And she knew it was true. She smiled into her father-in-laws eyes. Neither heard the entry door open, nor the hurried footsteps halting just beyond the threshold of the drawing room.

"Pop? Silvia?"

Silvia turned toward the familiar voice, shock replaced with a joy she never thought possible. "Victor," she cried before her eyes rolled back, and she collapsed at her father-in-law's feet.

* * *

She awoke, a cool cloth against her forehead, her head resting in her husband's arms. A feminine hand lifted the cloth replacing it with another.

"Is she all right? I never thought . . . . I didn't know."

"Yes, Mother. She's going to be just fine."

Monica began to fan herself, her face pink with concern. "No, my dear, don't try to get up. In your condition . . . well, you just can't be too careful."

You told? Silvia's wordless question prompted a smile from her husband as he answered, "Had to. Besides, Pop already suspected, and it was just a matter of time before Mother found out."

Silvia suddenly sat up, her eyes wide with love and shock. Victor was here, home . . . alive. It was the miracle she had prayed for. *Thank you, God. But—* "Where have you been? The letter—"

Victor ran his fingers through his hair, a tender smile on his lips. "I wanted to surprise you. I didn't even know about the letter until I arrived stateside. Do you remember Colonel Hawkins?"

"You mean, old Hawk-eye Hawkins, the terrible." She giggled, giddy with joy at her husband's return.

"Yeah," he grinned. "I ran into him at the bus depot. Boy, was he shocked to see me. He told me about the letter, and how I was supposed to be MIA. Somebody screwed up big time, somewhere. Anyway, he said he would take care of the mix-up, and since I was so near home, he thought it would be best if I just went on home, and saved the army the expense of sending out another letter . . . or something like that."

"But when you found out, why didn't you call?" She raised an eyebrow, scolding him slightly for his faux pas.

"I did, repeatedly, but you didn't answer. I was terrified something had happened to you."

She flushed. She had been so distraught over Victor's disappearance, it hadn't even occurred to her to plug in her cell phone. It lay silent and dead in the bottom of her purse. Oh, dear.

"When I got home, I searched the house from top to bottom, but I couldn't find you anywhere. Then it hit me that, being the adorable, honorable woman you are, you would have come *here* to my parents home to let them know . . . in spite of any, um, possible ramifications.

And I was right. Here you are, and here I am. I've got two whole weeks to spend with the woman I love. Glad to see me? "

In answer, Silvia threw her arms around his neck, clinging as if she would never let him go. Victor was safe, his parents knew, and everything was right with her world. No more secrets. No more grief. Just a miracle of love. And they lived . . . well . . . you know.

Spring 2002

SHE CAME, SHE WENT

She came, she went,
leaving chaos in her wake.
Tho young, she ruled the world.
After all, 'twas for her sake
the world was made –
or so she thought.

She came, she went,
and we cringed when she drew near,
for we knew, without a doubt,
everything that we held dear
would be destroyed –
before she left.

She came, she went.
We so hoped that as she grew
some changes would be made.
But in our hearts we knew
'Twas far too late
to save the lost.

4/7/99

TELL ME, BELOVED

Tell me, beloved.
You say you love me.
But do you really?
Is your love conditional?
Am I but a possession to you?

Your love seems strong when
you have your own way,
when you are in control,
but seems to dwindle
when I want mine.

Must there always be a price for your love?
Can you not love me
when my mood is less than perfect?
When I am less than perfect?
When I want to be myself?

What am I to you?
A mother?
A lover?
A child?

Tell me, beloved.
You say you love me.
But . . . do you really?

TERROR IN THE BAY

(Based on a true story
as related by Thomas L. Holbrook)

TOMMY WEAVER SAT alone on the shore hugging his knees as the incoming surf lapped at his toes wriggling in the damp sand—his spear gun within easy reach to his right, his only spear loaded and ready. His diving mask dangled from the tips of his index and middle fingers on his right hand as his left reached up to shade his eyes from the blinding sun.

It was relatively calm at the moment, and he was preparing himself for the first dive of the day. His grandfather wanted halibut for dinner and Tommy was more than eager to provide it, but his nerves were just a bit on edge, and he was waiting for his stomach to settle down before he ventured into the water.

This was his second summer vacationing with his grandfather at a small campsite on the Baja coast, and up until now he'd had no cares or concerns about anything. But that was before . . . before Manuel, the owner of the grounds, had told him all about morays and what they could do to an unsuspecting diver. Two summers ago a little girl had been viciously attacked while swimming in the bay, her blood-curdling screams slicing through the air as the eel wrapped its slimy body around her arm ripping and tearing her flesh to the bone.

She had been rushed to the hospital but it was already too late to save her arm—amputation at the shoulder . . . all that could be done. It wasn't until much later he discovered that it was all a lie. A lie fashioned to terrify a boy on the threshold of manhood. But today he believed it to be true, and so it was.

The bay was as full of terror as it was of beauty, it seemed. Just last summer his best friend, Jimmy, had been chased through the shallows by a 'monster shark.' He had barely escaped with his life. As he tumbled over the edge of the rented skiff, his left flipper, still firmly attached to his heel, remained bayside, gripped in the mighty jaws of the monster, pulling and twisting until the flipper gave way, slipping painfully over his heel and into the sea. Merrily munching on this odd tasting creature, the monster slowly turned and swam away. Of course, Jimmy was a jokester, so who would know whether it was really true or not, but—

Tommy patted the gun by his side as a nervous smile crossed his lips. After all, he did have his trusty spear gun. And Grandpa needed that halibut. Eel or no eel, shark or no shark, he was going to bring home the biggest halibut he could find. The problem was he would have to dive alone, and that worried him a bit. *Always dive in pairs . . . that's the rule. Watch each other's back . . . no one here to buddy with . . . gotta go . . . .*

The horseshoe-shaped bay beckoned, and he could resist no longer. He stood and stretched before slipping on his flippers. A gentle breeze wafted from the north creating a show of sparkling lights, as if a handful of diamonds and emeralds had been cast upon its surface. It was time.

As the waves reached his waist, he dipped his mask into the warm water before slipping it on, assuring a tight seal as he slid beneath the surface. Wearing a mask was like having tunnel vision. You could see only what was directly in front of you, and that only added to the teen's anxiety. Just to be on the safe side, he stayed away from any rock formations.

Carefully scanning the reef for any signs of halibut eyes, the only part of the creature not buried in the sand, he was finally beginning to relax, somewhat, when— Shark!

His heart raced, pounding in his ears, at the sound of the click, clickety-click of tooth against tooth, grinding, clicking in anticipation of a human meal. He whipped around, spear gun at the ready, but there was nothing out of the ordinary to be seen. He quickly scanned his surroundings, but finding nothing of any consequence cautiously went on his way. Click . . . clickety-click . . . .

Terror filled his eyes as he glanced over his shoulder expecting to see a gaping mouth full of spear tip teeth. But once again there was nothing unusual. Nothing until . . . . To his right, as if on cue, a shoal of shrimp swam by, snapping their tails to propel themselves backward. *Shrimp*, he laughed to himself. *Just a bunch of stupid shrimp. No eels. No sharks. Just shrimp.* He breathed a deep sigh of relief.

Moments later, he found what he had been searching for. Two large dark eyes peered out at him from the sandy bottom of the bay. He froze. This was it. *Halibut.* The biggest one he had ever seen. Slowly, ever so slowly he aimed and pulled the trigger— right between the eyes.

A perfect shot. *Oh, no*, he groaned at the dull thud that followed. His only spear had not only penetrated the huge fish but had pushed all the way through striking a rock and destroying the tip.

Heartsick, he pulled on the line preparing to haul his grandfather's fish to shore. But the fish did not move. He pulled harder and the ground began to shake. Grains of sand began to dance as two giant wing tips rose out of the sand and began to move—a slow rise and fall hauling the massive body from under a blanket of sand and into the warm waters of the bay.

The nine-foot angel shark began to undulate, flapping its wings, shifting its body from side to side, slowly towing the boy from the relative safety of the bay and into the unknown. The spear was still firmly entrenched between the false eyes near the shark's upper back. Tommy did his best to dislodge the spear, yanking, pulling and tugging, but was unsuccessful. He knew he should drop the gun and let the shark run, but it was the only one he had and there was no way he could ever afford to purchase another, so he held on tight.

He knew better than to turn his back on the shark, so facing forward and steeling his body, he allowed the animal to tow him around the bay. He had never felt such fear, and knew that if given half a chance the shark would turn on him, and that would be it. He'd never see his family again. Grandpa would have to go home alone and tell them . . . what? That he had let his grandson dive in shark infested water? Not a chance! He would just ride the shark until it tired and then bring it in. Shark fin soup sounded great right about then.

At last the angel tired of this game, and the cord towing our hero grew slack. *Great! I've got him now.* But as he pulled on the loose blue cord, the shadow at the bottom of the bay turned and was now facing him. Terrified, Tommy began to swim backward, spear still in hand. *Drop the spear,* his mind screamed, *and hide.*

But there was no place to hide, and the angel was getting closer by the second. Tommy reached for his diving knife tucked away in the sheath on his ankle. His arm stiffened, the blade held straight out in front of him, and waited. *Come on, shark. Come and get me. I'll slit you from your gills to well . . . all the way to gut city.*

Tommy's flippered feet moved slowly, back and forth, just enough to stay upright. He knew he couldn't outrun the shark, so all he could do was to stand his ground and pray for a miracle. The shark lunged and so did Tommy. He aimed for the shark's soft underbelly, but as he thrust, the angel's lower jaw dropped, and Tommy's left arm flew past the jaws and into the massive mouth. *Hey, this guy's got no teeth.*

He breathed a sigh of relief, and then grimaced in shock and pain, as the asphalt covered gums latched onto the shoulder of his wet suit and the angel rolled, twisted and ripped at his arm and shoulder. At last the rubber suit gave way and the triumphant shark slowly turned toward the open sea. Dragging the spear gun behind him, he swam away chewing aggressively on the skin of the 'seal' he had just peeled.

Tommy had never felt such pain as he struggled toward the shore. As he collapsed onto the safety of the beach, he felt as if his heart was trying to pound its way out of his body. His skin felt like one big nasty bruise, his left arm and shoulder bleeding with a severe case of 'asphalt' rash, but at least he was still alive and whole. Alive, but without . . . . He cried.

* * *

The golden seaweed swayed gently in the current at Garbage Row, a light blue cord tangled in its fronds, waiting . . . to be found.

THE BOSS

H E WAS SIX foot four, 285 pounds of pure muscle, and he was boss. From the time he was born, he knew he was destined to greatness, to control without mercy, those around him. It wasn't that he was a bully, for he was not. He just knew what he wanted, and how to get there, in the most expedient manner. As a child, he whipped the neighborhood children into shape, whether they wanted to be or not. He was a leader, a self-made man.

He soared in the workplace, rising in the ranks at an unheard of rate. And now he was boss, the absolute boss. He spent long hours at the office and demanded his subordinates do the same. They were expected to be at the office a minimum of fifteen minutes early, prepared to work; pencils sharpened, current project on their desk. Like a massive serpent, he slithered behind and between his employee's desks, constantly monitoring their progress, or lack thereof.

Break times were scheduled at fifteen-minute intervals, one worker at a time, lest they be consumed with trivial gossip. Perfection, as the result of hard work, was all he would accept. It was common knowledge that to be thirty minutes late or, Heaven help us, find it of necessity to leave a few minutes early, that employee's paycheck would most certainly be docked accordingly. Many would have walked, no run, to the nearest exit if the benefits would have been less. He was hard to work for, but the pay was better than elsewhere. So they stayed.

Then along came Marion. She slipped into the office, early one morning, silently, like a spirit, willing herself to near transparency, so no one really noticed her presence. She sat at the desk in the back corner, out of sight of prying eyes. Each day, thereafter, she was the first to arrive and the last to leave. She was painfully shy, so her social abilities lacked a great deal. While her co-workers took their breaks, she cowered in her corner, working all the harder to meet her quota. No one paid any attention to her, which was the way she wanted it, so her feelings weren't hurt . . . not really. Days passed, and she was happy in her solitude.

Then one day a shadow crossed her desk. Glancing upward, she gasped at the sight of the boss staring down at her. "It's your break time," he said.

"Oh, no. I couldn't," she answered. "I've much too much to do."

"Nonsense!" he declared. "Everyone needs a break—occasionally. You're working too hard."

Silence filled the room as pencils dropped and folders lay spread open on every desk. All eyes were on Marion and she blushed profusely. "Come, come," he said. "A cup of coffee will do you a world of good. You do drink coffee, do you not?"

"Well, yes, but—"

"Good. Come with me." He turned and strode with purpose toward the coffee room. Obediently she followed, hanging her head, again willing herself invisible, but to no avail.

It became routine, these coffee breaks, and Marion began to look forward to them. Every day he came to her desk, and every day they took their breaks together. The tension in the office lessened, and life became tolerable for the first time.

* * *

Marion doesn't work here anymore. You see she has a new job as wife and soon to be mother. The boss is still a taskmaster, but he rules with a gentler hand. After all, the love of a good woman can produce miracles even when it seems impossible. Thank you, Marion. We owe you one.

2/2/99

THE FISHERMAN

THE UNMISTAKABLE SCENT of bait and salt intermingled with the heavy, acrid smell of Diesel fuel. Seasoned fishermen roamed the deck, eager to cast out their lines. With the wind in their faces, they breathed in deeply, reveling in the coolness of the early morning hours, knowing the hot summer sun would soon be upon them.

The raucous cries of seagulls filled the air as they soared, bickering among themselves, then plummeted toward the unprotected bins of anchovies and chopped mackerel. "SHOO! You blasted thieves," shouted one of the deck hands. But they paid little attention to this insignificant human.

On the starboard side of the boat, a middle-aged man slouched in a faded blue and white deck chair, arguing quietly with his wife.

"I am deathly ill," he moaned. "I told you we shouldn't have come."

"You do look a little green. Did you take the Dramamine I gave you?"

"What Dramamine?"

"That little white pill I gave you before we boarded."

"I thought that was an aspirin."

"Well . . . did you take it?"

"No. I didn't have a headache."

"You *always* have a headache, whenever I ask you to take me anywhere."

"Well, not this time. I thought we were going to Catalina."

"We can go to Catalina anytime. How often do we get to go deep sea fishing?"

"I had hoped, never! O-o-oh . . . . I think I'm dying."

"You're not dying. Pick up a pole, and try to catch something. It'll get your mind off your stomach. Here, I'll even bait your hook."

"Don't bother. I just want to go home."

"Suit yourself, but remember, this is an all day trip. It's a long swim back to Dana Point."

"I think I really *am* going to be sick."

"If you think you're going to, do it over the side. I really would rather not clean it up."

"Such sympathy," he groaned, as he made a desperate lunge for the side of the boat.

* * *

The smooth oak railing felt somewhat comforting, and he clung as if his very existence depended upon it. *Twenty years with this woman*, he thought, *and she still doesn't know me.* He glanced quickly at his wife as she slowly let out her line.

"I'll get you for this," he muttered. "Just you wait and see. I'll get you for this."

* * *

She watched him with sadness in her eyes. For twenty years, she had cared for him, catered to his every need. It was always his way, or no way. For the sake of their marriage . . . their children . . . for *her* sanity . . . change must be made. It would be painful, but in the end, he would thank her. After all, if was for *his* sake she had braved the storm.

She raised her face to the heavens and took a slow, deep breath. She had never before asserted herself, and it felt good. She smiled, knowing her effort would be worth it in the end.

3/5/99

THE PIANO

Fine wood,
polished to a satin sheen.
Each grain subtly recognizable,
like fingerprints used to identify
a beloved child.

Strings,
so finely tuned,
the most critical ear
can find
no flaw.

Keys of ivory -
black and white,
eager to be caressed
by fingers more adept
than mine.

Music...
flowing, lilting,
resting upon my ear
like a fine wine upon the tongue
of a connoisseur.

Fine wood.
Finely tuned strings.
Ivory keys.
Music . . . flowing, lilting.
This . . . the piano.

SPRING 2002

THE PROMISE

I T WAS A glorious autumn day and it felt good to be alive. The air was crisp with the delightful taste of fall. The annual Harvest Festival had come at last, and the locals were out in great numbers.

Central Park was alive. People stood in family groups listening to the band play Gershwin tunes, and occasionally Sousa, which set the children to marching, marching, marching in time with the music.

Picnickers sat on old blankets or sheets (those which wouldn't be ruined if they received a little grass stain or two) spread with goodies of all kinds: cold fried chicken, potato salad, three-layer chocolate cake, a large basket of fresh fruit. And of course no picnic would be complete without the traditional old-fashioned lemonade—tart enough to pucker your lips, but sweetened just enough to satisfy.

* * *

It had been a hard winter and a devastating spring, what with the river flooding and all. But no one was killed, and things are just things, aren't they? Clean up and rebuilding had taken its toll, but eventually the land dried, as did the few homes at the

84

river's edge. It's strange how, in a crisis, something deep within the human soul pours forth and compassion seems to be the primary emotion—neighbor helping neighbor, old grudges forgotten.

It seemed the good Lord took pity on the town folk, and delivered a special blessing upon them, perhaps to compensate for their losses. A bumper crop they had that year. Some say it was the rich silt from the overflowing river, that made the difference, but most gave the credit to the Almighty, where it rightly belonged.

So now it was a time of celebration. And what better place to celebrate than the rich green of the park. Evergreens stood tall and proud, while the Maples, Aspens and Oaks prepared to drop their leaves. A slight breeze lifted the over-ripe leaves from their perches, sending them cascading to the ground below, weaving strands of brilliant color into the carpet of thick grasses.

"Look, Mommy," a child calls, lifting a fan of fallen leaves. "I made you a bouquet. Aren't they pretty?"

And the mother graciously accepts the bundle of color—reds, golds, purples, amber and yellow tinged with burnt sienna along the edges and lining each vein—holding them close to her heart.

* * *

He stood, leaning heavily upon the tree, watching his neighbors celebrate, tears coursing down his cheeks. This was not a happy time. He was alone—so alone. His mind drifted to that hospital bed, five years ago, where his only brother lay pale and weak, wires and plastic hoses everywhere. Leukemia, they had said. No chance. Too advanced. Just a matter of time.

"Promise me," the little boy had pleaded, barely able to speak.

"Anything," his brother promised, leaning closer to the dying lips.

"Please take care of Paco. Don't let him miss me too much." He coughed weakly before continuing. "And don't forget . . . to keep his wings clipped . . . so he can't fly away. . . 'till he gets . . . to know you."

"I will," he answered, tears filling his eyes.

"Don't cry." The little boy tried to be brave. "Just remember. As long as . . . you have . . . Paco, you will have . . . me too. I'm going to . . . Heaven now. I'm so tired. I'll wait . . . for you . . . there. Take care . . . of . . . Paco."

The teenager sobbed openly, his arm around his brother, his head resting on the pillow as his brother took his last breath. Then he was gone.

* * *

He tried to take good care of the redheaded parrot. They became good friends, but he kept Paco's wings clipped, just in case. After every molt, when the new flight feathers grew in, he carefully trimmed them just enough to keep him home. Then came the flood.

He thought Paco would be safe, at home in his cage, while he helped fill sandbags at the river's edge. How could he have known the river would reach his home? He found the empty cage, battered and bent, the cage door torn from its hinges, soggy green feathers plastered against the bars. The cage was floating upside down in the murky water, two blocks from his house. He grabbed it with his right hand and with all the strength he could muster, trudged homeward. The front door was open, mud and water flowing slowly from the doorway as it receded to the flooded street. Now he was alone, so alone.

* * *

Two elderly men stood in quiet conversation watching the sobbing younger man.

"He's a fool," stated one, matter-of-factly.

"Eh? What'd ya say?" asked the other.

"He's a darn fool. Look at that—a grown man crying over a dead bird. Pitiful. Pitiful and disgusting."

"A dead bird, you say? What kind of bird?"

"Lost a redheaded parrot in the flood. Was his brother's bird. Kid died. Leukemia, they say. But that's no reason to carry on so. The man's a fool."

"Y-yes," agreed the second man slowly, his mind taking him back to that day when King, his black Lab, dripping wet, carefully laid a soggy, half-drowned bundle of green feathers on his doorstep. He had carefully picked up the bundle, dried his feathers and laid him in front of the heater, not too close, just enough to warm and dry. He nursed that little bird back to health, and thanked the good Lord for sending him a new friend. *Could it be the same bird? No! The bird is mine. King brought him to me. I saved him. He's mine. Oh, dear. Did I remember to lock the cage door? What about the window? Did I fergit to close it . . . or not?*

"Where you goin'?" asked the first man.

"I just remembered something I forgot at the house. Gotta go." He turned away. "I won't give him up," he muttered as he hurried toward home.

"You're gettin' old, man," the first man hollered at his friend's back, then continued to stare at the younger man by the tree.

* * *

The young man slid slowly to the ground, at the base of the old oak, and wrapped his arms around his knees. A sense of peace filled him for the first time in months, and he began to watch with some interest the activity around him. His heart lifted as he felt the presence of his brother surrounding him. "It's all right," he seemed to say. "I'm still here. I haven't left you."

* * *

The old man watched with interest the change in the younger man. "Somethin's goin' on," he murmured. "Strange happ'nin's today. Must be the change in the wind." *What was that?* A flash of green. A splash of red. The old man watched as the younger man sprang to his feet, laughter filling the air as a small redheaded parrot swooped down and landed on the young man's shoulder, nipping playfully at his ear.

"Paco, oh, Paco. Where have you been? I thought you were dead." He lifted the bird gently from his shoulder, held him in both hands and buried his face in the soft feathers. Paco began to squawk at this unaccustomed behavior, stretched his neck to one side and nipped at the young man's cheek. Pulling back, the joyful young man offered his right hand to the parrot.

Bobbing his tiny head all the way, he waddled up the extended arm, making himself quite comfortable on the familiar shoulder. The young man raised his eyes toward the heavens and mouthed, *thank You*. And he was happy.

* * *

An elderly man stood on the outskirts of the park, his hand resting on the head of a large black Lab, watching the young man and his bird. "Let's go home, King," he said. "We're too late. There's nothing more to be done here." Sadly, he turned toward home, but the black lab shook himself free, and bolted for the old oak. "King! Come back here!" he commanded. But the Lab ignored him, so there was nothing left to do but follow.

As he approached the group around the tree, Paco began excitedly dancing from foot to foot before taking flight, landing lightly on the old man's head, gently teasing the thinning hair with his beak. Just as suddenly, he returned to the young man's shoulder and continued his dance.

* * *

Two men faced each other, one young, the other old. One smiled, and held out his hand. The other answered in kind. Two men, with nothing in common but a small green parrot, knew at that moment they were destined to be friends.

* * *

A small boy peers down from Heaven, and smiles. His task is done. Now he can rest, knowing at last, his brother will be all right.

Rest in peace, little one. Rest in peace.

1/21/02

THE ROSE

I T BLOOMED QUICKLY, the rose. Too quickly . . . and faded before its time. It had great promise, perfectly formed, lovely with a subtle, yet pungent, scent. Petal by petal, dropping, falling, as if some great frost had reached out with icy fingers to devour and destroy the very essence of innocence.

Her name was Rosalie and like the rose, had a delicate beauty seldom seen. I remember the day I first saw her. Her parents had recently moved into the old Douglas place next door, which seemed curious at the time. They had obviously lived a hard life, and who would have thought . . . the Douglas place . . . The property tax itself must have been half a year's salary. It wasn't until much later we found out the place was inherited, with a tidy monthly sum to help cover expenses.

They were nice enough folk, but somewhat drawn within themselves, if you know what I mean. However, they did dote on that child. She was their only one, you know, and lucky enough to get her, I understand. She could have been spoiled, but was somehow spared that terrible disease. A sweeter child you could never know.

She was born in that house, you know. Came so quickly, getting to the hospital was out of the question. Couldn't begin to make it on time. It was my birthday, and it seemed not one soul remembered. Not a card, not a call. Not a sound from anyone until that frantic pounding on my kitchen door. Knowing a bit about birthing, having had seven of my own, the Mister had come to get me, lickity-split, when it was time. She was three weeks early—a tiny little blossom, pink as the roses that bloomed in my garden. That's how she got her name . . . Rosalie.

We became great friends after that, the Martins and me, especially little Rosalie. My children had all left the nest, spread out across the country like seven blueberries set across a twelve inch pie. We seldom saw each other, 'tho they called occasionally, just to check up on me, they said. 'Tis a pity when lives become too busy to dream, or spend with loved ones.

Anyway, Rosalie became my 'adopted' grandchild - rarely getting to see my ones by blood. I called her my darling Rose, and I was 'Grammy' Sue. We celebrated our birthday together year after year. The only time my children came to see me was at Thanksgiving. I so enjoyed them when they came, but you know how busy life can be. Some weren't fond of having the Martins join us, but eventually accepted them as an inevitable part of our celebration.

Christmas, however, was spent at the Martin's. My children were too busy with their own Christmas traditions to include me, so the blessed season was spent with those closest to me, my neighbors. We were like four peas in a pod, happy to be together. We rejoiced in each other's happiness, and cried in each other's sorrows. We were family.

* * *

She grew up so fast . . . too fast. It seems only yesterday we laughed at our weekly tea parties, playing with teddies and dolls. Her favorite was a soft sculpture baby doll I had made especially for her. It was my first and so was not perfect. But perhaps that was why she loved it so. "Everyone needs to be loved, Grammy Sue," she would say. "Especially people like Charlie. He needs it a lot."

Charlie was the gardener's half-wit son. He adored our little Rosalie, protecting her in his own simple-minded way. He responded well to kindness, and Rosalie, being the only bit of kindness in his life, graciously accepted his adoration. "Charlie needs a friend," she would say, and I could not argue with her. The good Lord must have poured all of His best into our little Rosalie. She was gifted beyond measure, but never uppity or conceited. She loved everyone, and everyone, her.

"Slow down," I used to tell her. "You're growing too fast." And she would lay her head on my lap and smile. "I'll never be too old to love you, Grammy Sue. I'll always be there for you." And I would smile, caress her sweet face and answer in kind. But life has its own will and grow up she did.

I remember how happy she was as she swept through life and into young womanhood. How excited she was when her beau, Richard by name, invited her to the senior prom. She looked so beautiful that night - a starry-eyed, slender, perfect rosebud on the verge of unfurling, petal by petal. Unbeknownst to Rosalie, Richard planned a proposal of marriage on that very night. He was a good boy, that Richard, and would have made a good husband, but . . . .

* * *

I was awakened from a sound sleep, by fierce pounding on my front door. Alarmed, I threw on my robe and sped downstairs, fear clutching at my heart. I threw open the door and . . . there was my beloved Rosalie, laying in a heap, tattered and bleeding.

I gathered her into my arms, my eyes frantically searching for a clue as to who had done this dreadful thing to my darling Rosalie. And then I saw him. Crouching behind a Banks rose, terror in his eyes, his tee-shirt drenched in blood, trembled Charlie. I screamed.

The ambulance came.

"Gently," I cried, as they lifted her broken body, stiff with shock, and raced to the hospital.

The police came and took Charlie away.

"How could you," I screamed. "She loved you." But all he could, or would, say was, "I didn't mean to," over and over again.

* * *

The hospital room was deathly still as the doctor explained her injuries to us, her family. "There's nothing we can do, but wait," he said. And wait we did, hours . . . days . . . weeks, but she remained in a catatonic state. "It was just too much for her to bear," we were told. Innocence lost at the hand of a half-wit.

The jury found him innocent, or should I rather say . . . not guilty, because of his simple mind—a mind that did not recognize the consequences of his sinful, grievous act. So he was set free while my beloved Rosalie was kept a prisoner in her own mind. How I hated him for what he had done. I am sorry to say, as a good Christian woman, I once wished him dead. But who can fault a simple mind?

Oh, Rosalie, how I mourn for you and your unborn. Twins, the doctor says you are carrying. I pray daily they have inherited your grace, beauty and intelligence, and not the simple mind of their father. God help us all.

They brought Richard in, that horrible day, battered and bleeding, a knot the size of a hen's egg lifting the hair at the base of his skull. Found him staggering along the road leading into town. *They* called it a mugging, but *I* know who was really responsible. The poor, dear boy.

He was so devastated at what was done to you. "I'll never desert her," he vowed as he joined us in prayer. But his vow was short-lived as the weeks and months slipped by. He found another, and finally stopped coming altogether. Left town, I understand. He thought it best. He was right, I suppose.

So now we sit and wait . . . and wait . . . and wait—the Martins and me. We've waited such a long time. The babes are being delivered as we wait. Rosalie, my dear one, do not worry about them. They shall be cared for as if they were our own, half-wit or not. The doctor is coming. The babes must be here.

* * *

"They are beautiful, my darling Rosalie. Not at all what we expected. How I wish you could see them with your own eyes. You have born daughters, as lovely as the pink buds of roses in our garden. Can you hear their cry? These precious babes look just like I remember you the night you were born. Rosalie? Rosalie . . . Have you come back to us?"

The cry of the babes must have awakened something deep within her soul as she began to stir.

"Mama . . ? Grammy Sue . . ? Is that you . . ? Where am I?"

"In the hospital, dear. You've been here a long, long time," I said.

"Grammy Sue? I have some dreadful news to tell you . . . about last night."

"Don't worry, dear. We know all about it. You are safe and he has been sent away. He'll not bother you again."

"He . . ? He who?"

"Why, the half-wit who took your innocence, of course . . . Charlie."

"Oh, no, Grammy Sue. Charlie rescued me. It was Richard . . . only Richard. I would have died, had it not been for Charlie."

My heart sank as I realized what a senseless conclusion we all had come to. We should have known, but allowed appearances to deceive us. Charlie, the innocent. What had we done? Charlie, the simple minded, but pure of heart, forgave us all, and became a vital part in the lives of Rosalie and her babes. Richard disappeared, never to be seen again—guilt his only punishment. As the good Lord lives, so be it. 'Tis best that way . . . I suppose.

* * *

It is spring, and the roses are blooming profusely. Charlie takes good care of them, especially the pink one with the tiny pink buds just beginning to unfurl. Thank you, Charlie . . . for everything.

THE RUNAWAYS

MATTHEW SCOWLED, REPEATEDLY jabbing at the power button on his laptop.

"What's the matter?" his younger sister, Chelsea, asked.

"It quit. That's the third time this week. I should toss this piece of trash."

She knew Matt's sour mood wasn't just about the faulty computer; something else was bothering him, big time. It wasn't like him to snap at anything, much less an inanimate object like a computer. Since Mama died, two years ago, he had been her protector, her comforter, her best friend. But now . . . .

"Sorry, Chels. Guess I'm just a little uptight. I finally got a lead to where Dad might be, but this stupid computer shut off before I could get it written down."

"What are you gonna do? Did you find out anything at all?"

"All I know is he used to live in Bozeman. But that was three years ago, after he left . . . the last time. I just have to wait 'til it cools down, then I'll check again. I don't think the fan's working right." He turned the PC onto its side and tapped on the screen where the sluggish fan waited to be brought back to life once again.

"What happens when we do find him? It's not likely he'll want us living with him. He hasn't even tried to contact us since Mama died. Maybe he just doesn't care anymore." She shivered, as much with the situation as the cold. They had been standing and waiting for what seemed like hours, for the delayed bus to arrive, and now that it had, it was starting to rain.

Cold, miserable and uncertain. They'd be better off if they had stayed at the Martin's. At least it was warm, and . . . . Her stomach began to growl. "Why don't we just go home?" she whined. "I'm tired and hungry. Nothing's going right."

"We're not going back there . . . ever. You hear?"

"Why not? Aunt Linda's going to pitch a fit. We're supposed to be in school, not off to who knows where. It's not that I don't want to find Dad, but I don't think he wants to be found, and I'm cold, and tired, and . . . I want to go home. Aunt Linda . . . ."

"Don't call her that! She's not our aunt. She's just somebody the system decided to dump us with."

"Boy, aren't we in a great mood. She's nice, and so is Uncle Jake. I like him."

"Yeah," he snapped. "And he likes you too."

"What's that supposed to mean?"

"It means that he looks at you the way a mouse looks at cheese."

"He does not!"

"Listen, Chels. I'm almost seventeen, and I've seen that look before. Believe me, 'Uncle' Jake is not a nice person. Come on. The bus is loading." Slipping his bedroll over his shoulder, he grabbed the duffle bag, and with his free hand, dragged his sister to the bus. If Chelsea was getting cold feet, he needed to make certain she had no other choice but to stick with him. Settling at the back of the bus, he rummaged through his bag, and pulled out a baggie half-filled with several broken cookies. "Here," he said, as he handed them to his sister. "It's the best I can do for now."

"Thanks," she smiled, grateful for even this small offer. "Want one?"

"No, you eat 'em. I'm not hungry." He shut his eyes and leaned back against the seat, the purr of the engine lulling him to sleep.

Moments later the scream of sirens jolted him awake as a half-dozen patrol cars flew past.

"What the—" The driver swore softly as he flipped on the radio. The commentator's voice was clear, in spite of the intermittent static.

"There's been a murder in West Falls. Prominent businessman, Jake Martin, was found dead in his vehicle, three miles west of the city. The police are looking for two run-away teens, for questioning."

The driver glanced in his rearview mirror at the two kids slumped in the back of the bus. His eyes met the terrified gaze of the boy, who was slowly shaking his head.

EMOTION

SUMER 2007

CALIFORNIA GOLD

Golden child with golden tresses
playing on the golden sands,
building priceless, golden castles
with her tiny golden hands.

Seems like only yesterday
we watched our golden miss
turn doldrums into fantasy
and chaos into bliss.

Golden California beaches
line the shore 'twixt sea and land.
Crashing amber waves approaching
golden castles in the sand.

Hush my child, no time to weep,
'tis time for building once again
golden castles in the moonlight,
homes for fairies and their kin.

Golden child, dance in the moonlight,
skip across the golden sands.
How I long to kiss you, hold you,
once again with trembling hands.

Golden child with golden tresses,
angel wings will give you flight,
but don't forget your golden castles
paling in the waning light.

As I build *my* golden castles
here upon this golden band,
you will always be here with me
building castles on the sand.

PATCHES

ANNE STOOD AT the muddy edge of what had once been her perennial garden and stared at the devastation before her. Tears mingled with the tiny rivulets streaming from her rain-soaked hair, and she shivered as the cool morning air slipped through her saturated cotton blouse.

Gone . . . everything gone. A lifetime of memories destroyed in the time it took for her home to burn to the ground. She kicked at the charred remains of what had once been a rustic nameplate, painstakingly carved by her then nine-year-old son and carefully hung by the front door for all the world to see. A few embers still glowed, protected from the elements by the massive gray stone fireplace, now standing alone and unencumbered by stucco and plaster and wood.

"Why?" she moaned. "Why?" *Why don't parents teach their children not to play with matches? How many lives lost? How many homes?*

She was one of the lucky ones, she guessed. She had sent her family packing, with as much as they could carry, as soon as the evacuation alarm had sounded. At least *they* were safe. But it all happened so fast. Birth certificates . . . insurance papers . . .

teddy bears, and, in all the confusion no one had remembered Patches. Why didn't anyone remember Patches?

* * *

She was so tiny when they found her, huddled by the front door, shivering, with that plaintive mew that had so thoroughly won their hearts. Love at first sight, that's what it was. No bigger than a minute. She couldn't have been more than four weeks old. At first they had thought she must have wandered away from home, but since no one seemed to know to whom she belonged, she was quickly adopted. She had accepted everyone in the family, but the bond between Anne and the tiny calico kitten was immediate and certain. The two rapidly became inseparable.

Where Anne went, the kitten went. Where Anne slept, the kitten slept. Anne's pink fluffy slippers became the kitten's favorite mode of transportation until she grew too large to grip the fibers with her tiny claws and too heavy to be dragged along behind. For ten long years Patches had shadowed her mistress, her eyes shimmering with unconditional love. But now she was gone.

* * *

Anne had been the last to leave. Confident of her family's safety, she had stayed to hose down the roof. . . the evergreens. . . the gardens. But the fire came too quickly. She wasn't ready. She did her best, but . . . .

The fireman told her she had to go. It was her last chance for escape. As she slid into the driver's side of the old pickup, she glanced one last time at the house she loved so much. Her eyes widened with horror as Patches' small body appeared at her bedroom window on the second floor.

"Patches!" she screamed, as she struggled to release her seat belt. She could hear the terrified yowls as the roof burst into flames, quickly engulfing the attic, and moments later, the second floor.

* * *

So here she stood. The rain had come too late . . . too late. There was just a drizzle now. The clouds were all cried out, and *she* was emotionally drained. Her family couldn't bear to come . . . couldn't bear to see . . . .

She closed her eyes, isolating her mind, as one vehicle, and then another slowly sloshed by to homes somehow spared the devastation. She felt a tug on the hem of her blouse, and her heart skipped a beat.

"Mrs. Brown?" He tugged again. "Mrs. Brown? Are you okay?"

She struggled to gain her composure before turning to the little boy beside her. "Yes, Jimmy? What can I do for you?"

He unzipped his jacket and pulled out a tri-colored bundle of fur, a plaster cast covering one hip and long hind leg. "I found your cat. Thought you might want her back. She broke her leg, but it's fixed now. I—" But his words were lost as he and his precious bundle were engulfed in the grateful arms of the mourner.

And the sun shone once again.

1/29/02

LOST

MADELYN SLIPPED FEET first into the cool green water, her mind empty—her eyes devoid of life. She had thought about it for a long time, played with the idea of suicide, but had always dismissed it. After all, people who committed suicide never went to Heaven, always the other place. But even Hell was better than this. No one would miss her. Her family had disowned her, and to everyone else she was just a face in the crowd, a broken, bruised face, but still just a face.

She had thought she loved him. He seemed so kind and considerate at first. She knew it was wrong to move in with him, but he was so persuasive. "Just for a little while, until we see if we're really compatible or not." She had been reluctant at first, but she loved him so and he *had* promised to marry her. So she moved her belongings into the tiny apartment and started housekeeping.

Her family's disapproval saddened her, but she assured them everything would eventually work out. It was just a matter of time. Then the beatings started - just a slap across the face . . . the first time. Why, she had cried? He had apologized, said he had had a bad day at work, asked her forgiveness and promised—never again. He brought her flowers and when they made love, his tenderness wiped all the pain away. She didn't tell her family. They wouldn't understand. After all, it was just once.

Months later. Still no ring . . . . Unless you count the one around her eye. She stayed home a lot. She was ashamed. It had become a vicious cycle—beatings, apologies, lovemaking, round and round. She shouldn't complain. After all, it *was* her fault. She should have known he didn't like stuffed peppers. She could have kept the house a little cleaner, she supposed. But she was so drained. *What has happened to me*, she wondered. *I can hardly make myself get up in the morning.* Then . . . the visit to the doctor. *He* had insisted. "Get some pills. Anything to get you off your lazy butt," he had demanded. So she went.

Three months, the doctor said. Baby seems fine, but *she* has to take better care of herself. Exhaustion wouldn't do her or the baby any good. That was the day she told her family—the day they disowned her . . . forever. A child out of wedlock was a stigma they could not bear. She went home, wondering what *his* reaction would be. Would he be happy being a daddy? Angry? Would it matter at all?

"How could you let this happen?" he had demanded. "It's all your fault. You've ruined my life." Then he beat her and threw her out. Pregnant. Homeless. No place to go. No family, no home, no shelter . . . only the river.

She closed her eyes as she slipped deeper into the murky depths. 'But what about the baby?' a voice deep within her subconscious cried out. She opened her eyes. She felt her abdomen. *The baby . . . my baby. I have to live for my baby. Please God. Forgive me. Please don't let me die.* She struggled toward the surface, kicking and flailing. *I'm not going to make it*, she thought, her tears joining with the droplets in the river.

Strong hands . . . under her arms . . . lifting, pulling . . . breaking the surface of the water . . . *blue sky . . . air . . . life giving air . . . thank you, God.*

"Are you all right, miss? That was quite a fall. Thought you were dead."

She looked into the deep green eyes of the lone fisherman and smiled. "I'm all right," she whispered. And she knew she was.

THE ELEVATOR

I STOOD OUTSIDE THE Carlton Towers Savings and Loan as near to the curb as possible, just like my kid brother, Billy, and I used to do some twenty years ago. My neck ached, and I felt slightly light-headed as I strained to count the windows leading up to the 36th floor. It wasn't any easier now than it was then. Everything just kind of blended together after the 15th. I awoke from my reverie when I heard someone calling my name.

"Is that you, Mr. Simmons? They told me you was a comin'. I was that excited, I was. It's been nigh unto ten years since I seen you last. Here, let me get the door for you."

I couldn't help but smile at the old doorman's enthusiasm. It was good to see him again. I had been away too long. He walked me to the elevator, chattering all the way, then insisted on pushing the up button "for old time's sake." As the doors closed behind me, those last twenty years dissipated, and I was once more a twelve-year-old child riding up and down, up and down, for hours on end with Billy.

"Okay, Billy boy. Where would you like to go this time?"

"Take me to the moon, Tommy. Take me to the moon."

Up we'd go, straight to the 36th floor, then plunge back down to the first, hoping no one would stop the elevator, wanting to get on.

"Hey, Billy. Why do you like to ride up and down so fast all the time?" I asked.

"Be-cause . . . it makes me feel like I'm fly-y-y-ing," he grinned.

As the ancient elevator jerked to a stop, I was suddenly thrust back to the present. *Wish you were here, Billy,* I thought. *You would love this. It all looks just the same.*

The doors opened, and just for a moment, I thought I had stopped on the wrong floor. The entire room looked, and smelled, like a florist convention. There were huge floral displays, and potted plants everywhere. Row upon row of well-padded steel chairs stood stiffly in formation, like soldiers waiting to honor one of their own.

As old friends hurried to greet me, my eyes quickly scanned this great hall. There it was. A small table, framed with roses and daisies, cradled the picture of a smiling young Air Force pilot. *Billy,* I silently cried, my eyes filling with unshed tears. *You always wanted to fly. Who would have thought it would lead to your death. Billy, the hero, shot down over Viet Nam. It was supposed to be a rescue mission—a medical evacuation. Why did it happen? I guess we'll never really know. But I'm here for you, Billy. Just like old times. I'm here, brother.*

The memorial service was real nice, but I was glad when it was over. As soon as I could, I picked up Billy's picture, said my farewells, and headed for the elevator. As I went to push the down button, I could almost hear Billy's voice calling, "One more time, Tommy, one more time. Let's take her back to earth."

I stepped into that makeshift rocket ship, pushed the first floor button, and holding tightly to Billy's picture, plunged one last time to the ground below.

As I stepped out into the nearly deserted lobby of that huge old building, I was nearly flattened as two young boys flew past me and entered the magic of the elevator. I couldn't help but smile as I heard the youngest shout, "Take me to the moon, Danny. Take me to the moon."

HUMOR

3/4/99

CATS

Cats, cats, numerous cats.
There's so many of them
they're driving me bats.

Cats on the chimney.
Cats on the fence
yowling past midnight.
A dreadful offense.

Cats in the garden
stalking the birds.
Cats in the birdbath,
too many for words.

Cats, cats, cats everywhere.
Cats on the rooftop.
Cats on the stair.

Cats in the kitchen.
Cats in the den.
Oh, how I wonder when,
please tell me when

will these cats go away.
I just need one or two.
Three dozen's too many.
One mouser will do.

Kittens all over, now
aren't they so cute.
If they'd only stay little . . .
Oh, who gives a hoot.

2/21/99

COMIC CREATIONS

(Limericks)

1. There once was a man from Olathe,
   who had a great mole on his face - a.
   Though he tried to deny it,
   he just couldn't hide it,
   this mole on the man from Olathe.

2. There once was a student of writing,
   who stated "This craft is exciting."
   He took paper and pen,
   settled down in his den,
   and hoped he had adequate lighting.

4/11/99

FAIR OR UNFAIR

"Is it fair, or unfair, for my wife," said the man,
"to spend all her time at the Fair?
She should be home scrubbing the floors and the walls,
My supper she needs to prepare.

My pants need some mending. I can't find my socks.
This house is in marked disarray.
The garden needs tending. The faucet is broke.
These pictures need hanging today!

The bedroom needs painting. There's cracks in the walk.
The grass is two inches too tall.
The car needs repairing. The fence boards are loose.
Oh, doesn't she care at all?

Is it fair, or unfair, for my wife," said the man,
"to leave me with nothing to do?
She's off having fun, while there's work to be done.
If she doesn't do it, then who?

I've worked all my life for my children and wife,
and now it is time to retire.
It's getting quite cold. There's a storm coming in.
She should be home building a fire.

So I'll sit here and wait, and hope she's not late.
And pray I don't die in the mean'.
It'd serve her quite right, if she came home tonight,
to find a most horrible scene.

But what's that I hear? Is a car coming near?
Could it be my dear wife has returned?
Oh, Yes! What a wonder, she's come home at last.
And oh, what a lesson I've learned.

Well I've worked and I've slaved for our bacon and eggs.
But now that I've had time to think.
She's kept us together in all kinds of weather.
She should be in ermine and mink.

I've worked all my life for my children and wife,
but now I can see she has too.
"Twould only be fair, to do my fair share,
and do the things she's had to do.

So I'm changing my ways. 'Till the end of my days
I'll do the best that I can
to show how I love her and how much she means
to this stubborn, but grateful, old man."

1/19/99

THE APPLES

(A Think-About-It Story)

THERE WAS ONCE a man who, having eaten a juicy red apple, couldn't decide what to do with the core. It was too far to walk back to his house, he thought, and he certainly didn't want to litter his own front yard. So . . . carefully checking to make sure no one was watching, he carelessly tossed it into his neighbor's yard. Fortunately, for him, the apple core landed in a small crevice half-filled with dry, crumbled leaves. "Wonderful," he smiled with satisfaction. "Now no one will know what I have done."

Sometime later, the discarded seeds began to sprout. Soon tiny leaves were peeking above the ground. One day as the neighbor was working in his yard, he came upon the little tree. "Come and see. Come and see," he called to his wife and children. "The good Lord has sent us an apple tree to feed us in our old age. We must take good care of this special gift so it will grow and produce much fruit." The neighbor immediately cleared away the debris from around the little tree, and having dug a trench around the tree, watered it well.

For the next several years, the neighbor and his family cared for the little tree. They watered it, fed it, pruned it, and protected it from the cold. They even built a fence around it to keep the

118

animals from nibbling on the tender branches. The little tree was happy to be so well cared for.

One beautiful spring morning, the neighbor went out to see how the little tree was faring and found it covered with small white flowers. "Come and see. Come and see," he called to his family. "The little tree is rewarding us for all our hard work by producing many flowers for much fruit."

And sure enough, as the months flew by, the little tree produced such an abundance of fruit, its branches had to be propped up to keep them from breaking. The neighbor and his family dreamed of fresh apple pie and cobblers to eat, and sweet juice to drink. Then one warm summer day, the neighbor told his family, "The apples are ripe. Tomorrow we will harvest."

The family found it hard to sleep that night and woke before dawn eager to begin the harvest. But when they got to the little tree its branches were bare. Not a single apple remained. "What could have happened to all our apples," they cried.

Searching diligently this way and that, the neighbor soon noticed 'the man' eating a big red apple.

"Someone has taken all our apples from our apple tree," he said. "Do you have any idea who would do such a thing?"

"Yes," replied the man. "I harvested them last night."

"But why did you take our apples?" the neighbor asked. "Please return them."

"No," the man replied. "They're *all* mine. If you don't like it, take me to court, and I will prove to you the apples belong to me."

Confused, but not wanting to lose his delicious apples, the neighbor and his family went before the judge asking him to make the man return the stolen apples. Upon hearing the neighbor's story, the judge asked the man why he had taken the apples. The man replied, "Because they were mine."

"How can you say they were yours," the judge asked, "when your neighbor spent years caring for the little tree, and you did nothing?"

"Because," smiled the man, "I planted the seeds."

Think About It

1. What do you think the judge decided? Why?
2. Who do think really deserved to have the apples? Why?
3. If someone does something wrong, but it turns out to be good for someone else, do you think he/she should profit from it?

THE APPLES

(Part two)

"**A**HHHH," NODDED THE judge. "I see your point."

The man smiled smugly at the thoughtful judge, thinking to himself, *I am a clever man. The apples are as good as mine, with nothing from my own pocket. Foolish man, this judge.*

"Now . . . let me see," continued the judge, "if I have this right. You, unwise as it may seem, saw fit to trespass onto your neighbor's land and plant an apple tree for his enjoyment."

"Well, I—" stammered the man. "Not exactly . . . I—"

"Come, come man. Are you saying you did not trespass, or you did not plant the tree?"

The man began to perspire as he shifted nervously back and forth before the judge. "Um . . . . The seeds *were* mine, but I did *not* trespass."

"Then how could *you* have planted them?"

The man thought and thought. Suddenly he brightened and explained, "It was the will of the good Lord."

"The good Lord?" questioned the judge.

"Yes," smiled the man once again. "When the apple I was eating came to the core, I heard a voice, clear as day, say, 'toss it into thy neighbor's yard, and you will be greatly rewarded.' And so I did. I have accepted my reward with the abundance of apples He has given me."

The judge smiled and leaned toward the man. "I see you are a man of many words and have given me food for thought. I have made my decision. The verdict shall be as follows."

The man stood proudly, his head erect, and waited confidently for the judge to continue.

"I feel that even though you did not trespass onto your neighbor's yard, you did, by your own admission, toss the core—complete with seeds—into his backyard, which then became the property of your neighbor. I further find that without the diligent care of your neighbor and his family, the tree would quickly have ceased to exist, therefore providing *no* apples for anyone. The 'good Lord's' reward shall go to the one who, by the sweat of his brow, earned it.

"But you too shall receive a reward—one justly deserved. For one full year, you shall work for your neighbor, three days a week, without pay. One day a week, you will sweep the town clean, disposing of all litter from north to south and from east to west. And lastly, you shall return every apple stolen from your neighbor's tree, and pay him double the market price for those which you cannot return. This is my final word. So be it."

"But how can I attend to my own affairs?" he pleaded.

"You should have thought of that before you stole from your neighbors. My verdict stands."

The man looked so stricken, his neighbor took pity on him and begged the court's leniency.

"My verdict stands," said the judge to the neighbor. "But how it is implemented, I will leave up to you."

So, for three days of every week the man worked for his neighbor. But the kindly neighbor insisted on paying the man for the work done, not with coins, but with the fruit of his labors, in pies, cobblers, and juice, which so humbled the man, he repented of his misdeeds, and eventually became great friends with the neighbor and his family.

As time went on, the townspeople, seeing the change in the man, began to follow the example of the neighbor, and soon the village became known throughout the province as "the town of caring."

As for the cleaning of the town, the man received so much help from his caring neighbors, the village became a showplace, and the townspeople no longer needed to be ashamed. As visitors came from far and wide to see this special place, the coffers became full, and the village prospered, all because of an apple core, a kindly neighbor, and the verdict of a wise judge.

SPRING 2002

THE OLD MAN

"What's that I hear?" the old man said,
clasping the 'horn' close to his head.

"You say old Jonesy's gone and dead?"
"No, sir, I said his daughter's wed."

"You say the preacher's down and out?"
"No, sir, I said he's plagued with gout."

"Speak up, young man, make yourself clear.
You act as if I cannot hear.

If you would only speak more plain,
you'd save us both a lot of pain."

And so I do my best to speak
quite clearly, lest I seem too weak.

Still he complains from day to day,
and tells me to be on my way.

He'd rather hear what he hears best,
and live his life with zeal and zest.

But I just smile and nod my head
before I tuck him into bed.

NATURE

2/21/99

HAIKU

1. As chill winter's snow
covers the dead in the ground,
we long for new life.

2. The red squirrel stands
scolding, while gathering nuts
for winter's deep sleep.

3. The stately old oak
wilts in the hot summer sun,
longing for cool peace.

4/3/99

OH WHERE
CAN THE POOR BIRDS GO

Oh where, oh where can the poor birds go,
flittering, fluttering to and fro?
Diving and swooping with no place to land,
for cats and their kittens await on the sand
to gobble them up with nary a thought
for all the bird children who haven't been taught
to fly like the wind, when the wind doth blow.
Oh where, oh where can the poor birds go?

Oh where, oh where can the poor birds go,
when the wind sends them tumbling to and fro,
when their homes are exposed to the rain and the dew,
oh what, oh what can these poor birds do?
From cats and their kits, from wind and from rain,
won't someone please save these poor birds all this pain?
To save these dear birds on this cold wintry day
I guess I'm elected, seems no other way.

So I'll build them a haven far above ground,
where sunshine and water and fresh seeds abound.
Where there'll be no more worries of kittens or cats.
(They'll have to chase lizards, mouses or rats.)
And the wind and the weather won't mean a thing
to these small cozy condos. Just hear how they sing.
Now the poor little birds will have some place to go
flittering, fluttering to and fro.

SPRING 2002

THE DUNES

Grains of sand –
      scooped into ice-cream hills,
            formed by the hand, and breath of God.

Trickling sands –
      small creatures hunt and play,
            grateful for the coolness of the night.

Quiet sands –
      silence fills the night with
            restful peace until the morning comes.

Shifting sands –
      Dunes, pale in the moonlight,
            waiting the rising of the sun.

4/21/99

THE OLEANDER

What creatures lie beneath your sheltering cover of leaves,
nestled within the coolness of your moist roots,
grateful for a tiny respite from the burning sun?
Do they worship you? Call you savior?
Are you perfect in their eyes?

You do not need the shimmering shine of the holly or rose.
Your beauty lies within you.
The pastel buds of youth adorn your branches
bringing a modicum of color to otherwise drab lives.
But yet you also hold a fatal beauty in your verdant leaves.

Poison -

Like the sting of a serpent.
Leading to the path of death and destruction.

Like the forbidden fruit of Eden, death awaits
one who would eat of your leaves.
Tell me.

Are you friend or foe?
Shelterer or deceiver?

Caution!

I choose to look upon you as a beautiful friend,
comforter and hero of the
weak
and
small.

3/6/99

THE POND

Reeds rustle in the gentle breeze.
Cattails and pussy willows
                    shelter new life.
Wild flowers offer their nectar to bees,
while bull frogs sit croaking
                    calling for mates.

Dragonflies skim the water below,
          rippling its smoothness as they
gingerly touch the skin of the pond.
I follow a pathway overrun
          with vegetation, pole in hand,
      hoping to catch that
                              elusive
                              Grandfather catfish.
I sit with my pole, 'neath
a large willow tree, immersed in the life
                    that surrounds me.
I cast out my line.
It lands, not quite touching an overhang of rocks.

I wait and hope.
So shady and peaceful, I might
fall asleep, sheltered from
the humid heat of summer.
Each year I come
to this little known pond, hidden away
amongst the foliage and trees.
A secret place known only to
its inhabitants,
my grandfather, my father,
and me.

4/27/99

WHAT SHALL
I HAVE IN MY GARDEN?

What shall I have in my garden?
A birdbath with angel atop?
Grass covered, stone lined pathways,
There, beauty and grace never stop.

The iron gazebo fair bursting
with trumpets of pink, white and blue.
Masses and masses of flowers
in every bright color and hue.

Dahlias and larkspurs and pansies.
Zinnias, snapdragons galore.
Oh, what a riot of color.
I think I will add some more.

Flowers of beauty and stature.
Some tall ones, some middle, some small.
Fountains with crystal clear water.
Oh, won't I enjoy it all.

I guess I had better get busy
or my garden I never will see.
And when I am finished, I'll call you
to come over and sit with me.

Yes, I guess I had better get busy
or my garden will never get done.
And when you come over to visit
we'll have lots and lots of good fun.

We'll stroll by the hour through the garden.
And then when the day is through,
I'll pick a bouquet from my garden.
And then I'll present it to you.

My best friend.

ROMANCE

1/31/99

CLOUDS

THEY SAT AND watched the clouds go by, just like it was any other day.

"How fast do you think they're going?" he asked.

"Pretty fast," she answered. "Probably fifty miles an hour."

"Yeah," he sighed, "just like my life. One minute you're there, the next – you're just a memory. And then, who knows . . . probably forgotten all together."

"Oh, come on. Lighten up. Nothing can be as bad as all that. Besides, who could ever forget you?"

"Marsha, for one."

"Marsha, who?"

"Marsha, *who*? The love of my life. The one who makes life worth living. *My* Marsha."

"Oh. *That* Marsha. See? I've forgotten her already. But you— You are an unforgettable character—handsome, charming, witty. A great all-around guy."

"Don't try to make me feel better. It won't work."

"Sheesh . . . . There's a lot more to life than Marsha. For instance . . . look at that cloud up there. What do you see?"

"I see . . . Marsha, riding her bike on the way to school."

"Wrong! That's a hippo on a motor scooter. What about that one over there?"

"Marsha," he sighed once again, "getting ready to spike a volleyball over a net."

"Wrong again. It's a sea lion, trying to balance a ball on her nose," she laughed. "See? It's all a matter of perspective. By the way, what did *Mar*-sha do to get you so down?"

"She decided to go to the prom with somebody else."

"Instead of you—Mr. Wonderful? She must have rocks in her head. What exactly did she say when you asked her?"

"Nothing."

"Nothing? How rude!"

"Not really. I hadn't had the time to ask her yet."

"You're kidding. Even so, since she's your girl, she had no business agreeing to go with someone else without at least breaking up with you first."

"Well," he shifted nervously. "She isn't exactly what you'd call *my* girl. In fact, she probably doesn't even know I exist."

"Of all the—"

"I know. I know. Just leave me alone, and let me die in peace."

"I can't believe you put yourself through all this. So what if she's going with someone else? You can still ask someone, too."

"It's too late. The dance is tomorrow. Everybody's already going that is going."

"Ha-hum," she cleared her throat.

He turned to stare at his best friend, "You wanna go?"

"I thought you'd never ask." She sprang to her feet. "Gotta go. Pick me up tomorrow at . . . 8:00, and don't be late."

"Well, I'll be," he grinned. "Who would have thought? Just wait 'till Marsha see us . . . . Marsha . . . ? Marsha, who?"

4/27/99

COULD THIS BE LOVE?

I see you there.
So far away,
and yet so near.
I can almost reach out and
        touch you.

Where are you, so far away?
What are you thinking?
Who are you thinking of?
I see how your eyes seem to be searching,
        diligently, but secretly,
                for something or someone.

No one sees but me.
Could it be her?

I see her tiny, secret smile
whenever you enter a room. Then
I watch her quickly check to make sure
no one is watching.

I smile.
No one sees but me.

Could this be love?
When you shake her hand
      you hold it just a little longer
                    than necessary.

No one seems to notice
      but me.
Could this be love?
I see it in your eyes.

Go to her. Tell her.
Before it is too late.
Could this be love?
Don't waste precious time.
You only have . . . an eternity.

2/20/99

MY ONLY LOVE

We're growing old, my love.
        Just see how life has changed.
                My first, my only love.

When we were young, my love,
        and starting life anew,
                I knew, 'twas only you.

The tiny souls we bore,
        such happiness they brought.
                Such love, such perfect love.

We watched our children grow,
        and blossom into youth.
                Such loving, caring souls.

We watched them one by one
        begin to leave the nest,
                to find their own true love.

We've been so very blessed
  each precious grandchild see.
    We watch them bloom and grow.

A little humor in
  our lives has kept the joy
    within our hearts, my love.

We've been through thick and thin.
  More thick than thin, I fear.
    The more to love, my dear.

Some may have wondered why
  I chose to spend my life
    with you, my only love.

To forsake any others,
  and say the big I do
    to you, and only you.

We're growing old, my love.
  No other could I choose.
    My first, my only love.

2/22/99

(A) POEM OF LOVE

How can I resist the smile
of one I hold so dear?
Committed for a lifetime
to have, to hold, to cheer.

In sickness or in sorrow,
it pleasures me to give
a helping hand, a loving touch
and with my lover live.

Your charming smile, your laughing eyes,
your loving, warm, embrace.
I only have to think of you
when life's too hard to face.

Without you dear, I'm torn apart.
But with you, I am whole.
I hold you deep within my heart,
and deep within my soul.

In good times, or in bad times,
my love will still be true.
I plan to spend eternity,
and more, in love with you.

SACRED

2/25/99

A PORTION

A portion of my life, Lord, I gladly give to you.
I'd give it all, but Lord you see, there's things I want to do.

A portion of my heart, Lord – I've saved some room for you.
I'd give it all, but Lord you see, I need a room or two.

A portion of my time, Lord - some moments, just a few.
I'd give you more, but Lord you see, I've got so much to do.

A portion of my money - I think a tenth should do.
I'd give you more, but Lord you see, I've obligations too.

A portion of my love, Lord - I hope this much will do.
I'd give you more, but Lord you see, some others need it too.

A portion of my soul, Lord? I'd better think this through.
Eternity's forever, and Hell will never do.

A portion of my life, Lord? I give it all, 'tis true -
for I'd rather spend eternity in fellowship with you.

2/20/99

GOD'S HANDS

Those hands
Strong hands
Calloused hands
God's hands

Those hands
Caring hands
Loving hands
God's hands

Those hands
Kind hands
gentle hands
God's hands

Those hands
Healing hands
Helping hands
God's hands

Those hands
Meek hands
Mighty hands
God's hands

Those hands
Heavenly hands
Holy hands
God's hands

Thank you God, for holding me,
for lifting me, for loving me,
when I've needed you most
and always.

SUMMER 1997

SPRING PRAISE

One day while strolling through my yard
   in early spring, in early morn.

I spied a diamond drop of dew
   Upon a rose bud, newly born.

I heard a robin sweetly sing.
   "Arise, give praise unto the King!"

The One who formed that perfect rose,
   the drop of dew in sweet repose,

who gave the robin voice to sing.
   So too shall I His praises bring.

Then some sweet day on Heaven's shore
  I'll reign with Him forevermore.

And there through Heaven's gardens grand
  My Lord and I'll walk hand in hand.

2/16/99

THE OTHER SON

My heart is black.
      I burn within.
My brother has returned.

For many years
      he stayed away.
Our father's love he spurned.

He lived a life
      of wine and song.
With prostitutes he lay.

When penniless,
      his fickle friends
deserted him one day.

It served him right,
      when he was forced
to eat and sleep with swine.

He dreamed of home -
      what used to be,
and coveted what's mine.

I'll head for home,
      my brother said,
and with my father plead-

to be a servant
      in his house,
to fill his every need.

So he departed
      from that land
Not caring how I'd feel.

His only thought
      was of himself,
his wounded pride to heal.

My father saw him
      from afar. Rejoiced
when he drew near.

His robe, his ring,
      he placed upon
this wanderer, so dear.

He welcomed him with
      opened arms.
The fatted calf did kill.

A banquet was
      prepared for him,
his empty stomach fill.

I will not go
      into the house
his merry making see.

I've worked, I've slaved,
      but never had
a party thrown for me.

He squandered his
      inheritance,and
now he wants what's mine.

My father says,
      rejoice, my son.
All that I have is thine.

And then he pleads,
      forgive, my son,
and with your brother dine.

Forgive, I must,
      but not today.
The fatted calf was mine.

SKETCHES AND OTHER PROJECTS

PORTRAIT OF A TEENAGE GIRL

S HE WALKS INTO the classroom, almost unnoticed, her books held close to her chest. She places her books on her desk and slips quietly into her seat. Her dark chocolate eyes dart around the classroom. She appears alert, and aware of her surroundings. She rarely speaks, but when she does, her Hispanic heritage flows through.

Her hair is an unusual shade of medium brown, neither dark nor light, with a slight reddish tint and a sheen of burnished gold. It is so shiny the ceiling lights are reflected in its strands. Her bangs are straight and long, almost covering her well-shaped eyebrows. Her hair flows gently over her shoulder, and she twists the ends around her finger before releasing them to answer the next question on her history worksheet.

Her mouth is small, but full, her skin a soft, creamy tan, her cheeks and lips barely pinked. She rarely smiles, but when she does the slight imperfection of her front teeth is somewhat noticeable, as if she has too many teeth for the size of her mouth.

She wears very little mascara; her eyelids shadowed a pale blue-gray. She scrunches over her desk, making it difficult to read the blue and white Spanish words printed on her long-sleeved teal shirt. Her pale-blue jeans have a manufacturer's hole in the right knee, black tights peeking through the shredded material. More than a dozen bracelets—some beaded, some corded, some metallic—cover her left wrist and forearm.

Occasionally she lifts her head, her expression blank, as if in deep thought.

She glances at her watch—a cat's head, which appears large and cumbersome for such a slender frame. A wide brown circlet holds the watch snuggly to her right wrist. She squirms. It is almost time for class to end. She writes faster. She seems intent on finishing her work before the end of class. As the bell rings, she grabs her books, and hurries toward the door, pausing only to give a quick hug to a student just entering the classroom. She waves good-bye, and disappears.

12/13/2010

REFLECTIONS OF A TEEN

WE HAD A sub today. She was okay, but I miss Mrs. Blair. Ms. Winslow, the principal, said she won't be back for over a month. A month. That's a long time. She had her baby yesterday . . . a boy, I think. I hope she's happy. She wanted a girl. She already has two boys, and now another one? I wonder what's it's like—having a baby.

Sheila would know. She reads a lot, and being pregnant, she needs to know what to expect, I guess. She showed us her sonogram this morning in History. I couldn't tell what anything was, but she pointed out the baby's head and hands. It was so cool. It's a girl. I hope Mrs. Blair isn't sad she didn't get a girl.

I don't want to get pregnant until I'm married. It's okay for Sheila, I guess. Jose says he'll marry her, and take care of her and the baby, right after graduation, but things change . . . people change. I wouldn't want to put my baby through that.

Nobody understands my feelings except for maybe my mom. The boys in our school seem to think that if a girl will go out with them, she's looking for a *good* time. Except for Miguel. He's nice and respects girls. We've been best friends since Kindergarten.

The Saint Patrick's Day dance is next week. I wish Miguel would ask me to go with him. Mom says I'm pretty, and any boy would be privileged to take me to the dance. She would trust Miguel to take me out. But he doesn't think about me like a girl. I'm just like a little sister to him. Mom offered to ask Miguel's mother to ask him to take me to the dance, but I told her no. How embarrassing. I'd rather die.Someday, maybe, I'll get married, maybe even to Miguel. But things would have to change a lot for that to happen. And maybe I'll even be a teacher like Mrs. Blair, and have three kids, but one of them better be a girl.

THE JOURNAL (El Diario)

"MOM!" ARLENE SHIFTED from foot to foot, her hands spread along the back of the sofa, trying to determine which way her little sister might run to avoid being caught and relieved of the book she held possessively against her chest. "Mom!"

Mrs. Ramirez rushed into the living room only to discover her daughters in an apparent stalemate, her younger daughter smug, as she stuck out her tongue and then grinned at her frustrated older sister. "What's going on here?" she asked. "What did she do this time?" She sighed, and gestured, with her head, toward her eight-year-old, Carlotta.

"She broke into my room and stole my journal. Make her give it back."

"Carlotta?"

"I didn't break in. The door was unlocked. I just looked to see if Arlene was in there. That's all." She quietly slipped the journal behind her back. "She wasn't there so I left. Honest."

"Mo-om."

Mrs. Ramirez held out her hand. "The book, Carlotta."

"What book?" Carlotta asked, feigning innocence.

Her mother sighed. "The one behind your back. Hand it over . . . now."

"But, Mama."

"No buts. Just hand it over."

Carlotta pulled out the journal, once again pressing it close to her chest, an impish grin on her face. "Do you want to know what's in it?" she asked, eager to tell. "Arlene's in love . . . with Miguel," she giggled. "She wants him to take her to the dance, and—"

"You . . . you . . . ooooo." Arlene flushed, dove over the sofa and wrested the journal from her sister's grip. "You had no right, you little—"

"Arlene!" Mrs. Ramirez stared at her normally docile daughter. "What's got into you? And you, young lady," she turned to scold Carlotta, "know better than to—"

"*Silencio!*" The screen door slammed. "Do we have a problem here? Do we need to share our difficulties with the entire neighborhood? Mama? Que pasa?"

Mrs. Ramirez was quick to fill in her husband. He turned toward his youngest daughter. "Carlotta, I'm disappointed in you, *mi corazon.*"

"But . . . but . . . ." Carlotta burst into tears and fled to her room.

Crocodile tears, ran through Arlene's mind, as she hugged her journal and watched her sister disappear into the hallway. Her parents slowly shook their heads and sighed.

"Um . . . Mom?" Arlene turned toward her parents. "Miguel's coming over this afternoon to study for awhile. Can you please make sure Carlotta stays in her room and doesn't bother us? I'll just die if she says anything to him."

"I can try." Her mother breathed in deeply. "I will do my best to keep her busy while he's here. But you know how she is. She really does mean well, you know. Perhaps if you spent a little more time with her . . . no . . . I suppose not."

Mrs. Ramirez walked back into the kitchen to think about preparing dinner, while Mr. Ramirez went back to the garage for a little peace and quiet. Arlene stood alone in the empty living room for just a moment, before racing to her room to hide her journal. It would *not* happen again. She grabbed her books and spread them out on the dining room table. Miguel could be here at any minute, and she wanted to be ready . . . before he arrived. She glanced at the crucifix on the dining room wall. *Please don't let Carlotta ruin the day*, she silently prayed. *Please.*

* * *

Carlotta was on her best behavior. She opened the can of frijoles, dumped them into a microwave-safe bowl, and set it on the kitchen counter. She rinsed out the empty can of enchilada sauce, and threw it in the trash. Dinner was almost ready, and she was bored. Miguel and Arlene had been studying for almost an hour and she had not bothered them even once.

"All right, Carlotta, you may go get washed up for dinner. You've done a good job."

Carlotta grinned at her mother. "Can Miguel stay for dinner?" she asked innocently.

"I suppose, if he wants to. I'll call Margarita and ask if it's okay," she murmured absently.

"Can I ask him?"

"Sure, sure. Just don't bother them while they're studying."

* * *

Carlotta leaned her elbows on the dining room table, and rested her head in her hands. She stared at Miguel, a wistful smile on her face.

"What are you doing?" Arlene hissed, annoyed at her sister's obvious adoration of *her* best friend.

"I'm waiting until you guys get done to invite Miguel to stay for dinner. Mama said I could. Well?" She stared at Miguel.

"Well, what, little one?"

"Do you want to stay for dinner, or not?"

"Well . . . sure, if it's okay with your mom. I'd have to call home and—"

"No you don't. Mama already called. You can stay if you want to."

"Okay. That okay with you?" He turned to Arlene.

"Sure," she replied, giving her sister a 'what are you up to now' look.

"Okay then, I guess I'm staying."

"Miguel?"

"What, *hermanita*?"

Carlotta wasn't certain she liked to be called little sister, but under the circumstances—it would have to do. "Are you gonna go to the Saint Patrick's Day dance next week?"

"Well . . . I haven't really thought about it that much. Why? Are you asking for a date, *pequena*?" He winked and tapped the tip of her nose. "I think I might be just a little too old for you, but thanks for asking."

"Oh, I wasn't asking for me. I was just wondering if you were going or not?" She ignored the panic spreading across her sister's face. "Would you go if you had somebody to go with?"

"Well, I don't know. Maybe. Got anybody in mind."

"Do you?"

"I don't know. I—"

Carlotta breathed out a huge breath of exasperation. "How about Arlene? You could take her."

Arlene felt herself redden, and she sank deeper into her stiff-backed chair. She was going to die, but she would *not* die alone.

"Arlene? She wouldn't want to go out with me . . . . Would you?" he asked, turning to face her.

Arlene flushed but was unable to answer, her mind churning with discomfort.

"Good. Then it's all settled." Carlotta grinned at her sister. "I gotta go get washed up for dinner. Don't worry. I'll be right back."

* * *

Arlene stood by her sister's bedside and watched her as she slept. It had been the best night of her life, and she had her little sister to thank for it. The dance had been wonderful, and she had felt so beautiful in her shamrock-green dress and matching pumps. It was so much fun. Miguel had even asked her out for another date.

She lightly touched her bottom lip, still tingling from her first good-night kiss, and smiled. She sat down on the edge of her sister's bed and gently brushed the hair from her forehead with her fingertips. "Thanks, Carlotta," she whispered. "You're the best."

Carlotta snuggled deeper under her covers and smiled, a small book clutched tightly to her chest.

10/15/2010

MONSTERS, EGGS,
AND SWEET POTATO VINES

(A Childhood Memory)

I GUESS YOU COULD call it a utility room, but it's more, much more, than that. It's like a huge indoor sun porch, with windows covering one entire side, and part of another. A bushy-green sweet potato, in a tall glass jar half-filled with cool, clear, water, sits on a windowsill in the middle of the wall. Its vines, curled and twisted, are secured to small nails hammered into the tops of the window casing.

Every few inches a part of the vine tumbles free, giving the appearance of a lacey emerald valence covering the top few inches of the window. There are no curtains, other than the vines, so the room is always light and airy, at least during the daytime. I love how the sun shining through the vines covers the wooden floor with dancing shadows.

Anything that can't be stored in another part of the house ends up in that room, including not one, but two, refrigerators, snuggly placed against the windowless wall, one for kitchen use, the other for the amazing job of holding eggs, but not just any old eggs. My grandfather raises Banty chickens, and when he wants to save enough fertile eggs for the hens to set, he keeps the eggs in the 'just-cool-enough' second refrigerator.

The utility room holds many wondrous things, including a mated pair of parakeets. My grandfather constructed their plywood and wire-mesh cage, complete with nest-box. During breeding season, he carefully removes each newly laid egg, and replaces it with a hand-warmed marble of approximately the same size, until all the eggs have been laid. Then, when it's time, he carefully replaces the marbles with the 'real' eggs. This way all the chicks will hatch at the same time. If I am very quiet, he lets me lift the lid on the box and take a quick peek inside.

Not far from the nesting-birds hangs a square, wire cage with a very musical, yellow and orange canary. He sings day and night. It doesn't matter when. Oftentimes I find my grandfather standing next to his cage, whistling a duet with the tiny bird. The canary sings whatever warbles from his tiny throat, while my grandfather harmonizes in his own special way. I love to hear them sing. It's so beautiful and peaceful. But on laundry day, everything changes.

The washing machine looks innocent enough with its cool white enamel and small silver tub, but on Laundry day it comes alive. It's excruciatingly loud and sometimes rattles the floor with its quaking. The sweet smell of birdseed is replaced with the choking scent of powdered detergent, the small particles in the air sour, and acidic, on my tongue. But the most terrifying aspect of all is the wringer—two long, fat, rollers set so tightly together, if you get too close, your hair could get ripped out by its roots, or you could lose your fingers or an arm or . . . . At least that's what Grandma always says.

This is my favorite room, where I can sit in the old rocking chair and read, or think, or watch the sunlight making shadowed pictures on the wall. I love it most of all, because . . . it's a place where I can just be me.

11/20/2010

RED EYED TREE FROGS –
A RAINFOREST TREASURE

YOU ARE TIPTOEING through the Central American neo-tropical rainforest and it is getting dark, but you aren't worried. You have a flashlight in hand, and a guide beside you. Suddenly you hear a cacophony of sound. Chock. Chock. Chock. Hundreds of tiny frogs, croaking to their heart's content. The high-pitched sound you hear is the mating call of the male Red-eyed Tree Frog.

You flip on your flashlight and directly in front of you are two huge red eyes. Well, huge for a three-inch-long tree frog. The little female tries to climb away, but you see another smaller frog attached firmly to her back. It's breeding season, but there are no *Do Not Disturb* signs anywhere, so you stop and take note.

Oops. Where did she go? You hear a splash. You turn your flashlight to the marshy pool in front of you and watch as the little female sucks water into her bladder and begins the long climb back to the leaf she has chosen to lay her eggs. She struggles to maintain her balance as she extends one colorful leg in front of the other, carefully gripping the slippery stem. The tiny male is still attached, although other males have tried to wrestle him off and take his place.

This process of reproduction is called *amplexus*, which means the male latches onto the female's back, and fertilizes the eggs as they are laid, outside of the female's body. The eggs are laid in a watery, gelatinous mass on the underside of a leaf, called a clutch. The female lays three to four clutches in a time period of up to several hours. To keep her eggs from drying out and dying, she must drop back into the water to refill her bladder after each clutch of eggs is laid.

The Red-eyed tree frog is one of the few frogs to do this. Other frogs lay their eggs in ponds or small pools of water.

It takes six to eight days for the tadpoles to hatch; however, the irregular vibrations from a predator, such as a bat, a bird, or a slithering snake, can cause the eggs to hatch thirty percent faster than normal. When it is time for the eggs to hatch, all the tadpoles break out of their shells at the same time. With predators in the water, as well as the trees, this insures the best chance of survival for the tiny tree frog tadpoles.

A sudden breeze rustles the leaves forming the canopy, high above the rainforest floor; the sweet scent of a storm rapidly approaching. You lift your face and stick out your tongue as the first droplets begin to fall, cool, and soft, and delicious. It begins to pour, but the tiny frogs take no notice. Now you understand why it's called the rainforest.

Your guide suggests you leave and return at another time. You reluctantly agree, but before you go, you can't resist the urge to lift the edge of a nearby leaf for one last peek at what might be hidden there.

Plop, plop, plop. Dozens of tiny brown tadpoles drop into the water and disappear. Was it time to hatch, or did the vibrations from your hand cause premature hatching? It doesn't really matter, does it? A new generation has been born, and you have been a witness to it. It is time to go home, but you can't help wondering what it would be like to take with you just a few of the tiny tadpoles. Would they make good pets?

Hmmm . . . perhaps it would be best to leave them in the rainforest, where they can live and grow; from tadpoles to froglets and hopefully to adult tree frogs, starting the process all over again.

The red-eyed tree frog is one of the most colorful of all frog species. For such a small frog, it is striking, with a multitude of color. Although there are many combinations of colors, the most common is as follows. The head and back are iridescent green, the belly tan or cream colored. Their sides are purplish/blue with yellow stripes, and their legs are a fascinating combination of blue, purple, orange and yellow, with bright red-orange feet to match their bright red eyes. Suctions cups on the bottom of their toes enable them to climb trees, or hang hidden from predators on the underside of leaves.

Agalychnis callidryas (pronounced a-gali-chin-is cal-le-dry-as), the scientific name for the red-eyed tree frog, is the most popular frog in captivity, partially due to those massive red eyes, and colorful bodies, and partially due to their docile nature. However, they are very delicate, and only those experienced in their care should attempt to house them.

They require a tall, well-planted vivarium, with lots of climbing and jumping space. Native to the rainforest, the humidity level must be kept between 80-100%. The tree frogs will need to be misted everyday as well. A heat level of 78-88 degrees must be retained during the daytime.

Red-eyed tree frogs should not be handled, as the oil in your skin can harm them.

And finally, the tiny tree frogs are nocturnal, which means they will only be active at night. So, unless you are prepared to stay up late to observe them, using a red light, they will not easily be seen.

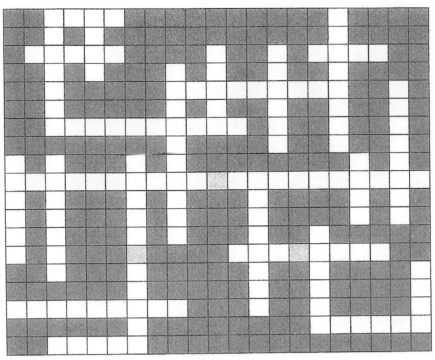

4 LETTER WORDS

BATS
EGGS
FROG
PLOP
TREE

5 LETTER WORDS

BIRDS
CROAK
WATER

6 LETTER WORDS

CANOPY
CLUTCH
LEAVES
SNAKES

7 LETTER WORDS

BLADDER
TADPOLE

8 LETTER WORDS

AMPLEXUS
COLORFUL
DELICATE
RED-EYED

9 LETTER WORDS

IRREGULAR
PREDATORS

10 LETTER WORDS

RAINFOREST
VIBRATIONS

11 LETTER WORDS

CHOCK-CHOCK

21 LETTER WORDS

AGALYCHNIS-
CALLIDRYAS

'TIL THE FAT LADY SINGS

AVE YOU EVER heard the saying, "It ain't over 'til the Fat lady sings?" Well, it's true. I know because I live it every day. My mom's a really cool person, but she's at least 150 pounds overweight. She says she has a thyroid problem, but I don't see her pushing away that second bowl of ice cream. It's embarrassing . . . totally. I can't even have my friends over. They might say something. I don't think I could handle that.

Mom used to sing for the Met (the one in Charleston, not New York), when she was younger, until she married Dad, and got that 'thyroid' problem. Dad's cool. He sings too, but not like my mom. She's good . . . but . . . let's put it this way, she doesn't need a microphone . . . no way. When we were kids and it was time to come home, you could hear her calling and calling, in this high-pitched sing-song she calls vocalizing. I bet you could hear her two miles away, without even half trying.

I guess what I'm *trying* to say is . . . I'm ashamed of my own mother. I know it's not right, but I can't help it. I don't even let her know when there's things going on at school, like my track meets, or performances, or anything. It's not like I want to be this way. I just am. I can't help it. It would be different if she even tried, but that's like trying to teach a cat *not* to like milk.

Today she's making me take her to 'the Met,' downtown. She wants to see her old 'stompin' grounds.' Maybe I can wear a bag over my head, or something. I just hope nobody sees me. I'd rather die.

* * *

Whoa! This is huge. It must fit . . . well, a ton of people. And my mom sang here? The thing I notice the most is how quiet it is. The only sound in the whole building is Mom's high-heeled shoes click, click, clicking away. I don't know why she wore those. She's going to turn an ankle, then who's gonna get her out of here? I'm lost in my thoughts.

"David? David! Please don't dawdle. I need to find my dressing room and sit down. My feet are killing me. Be a good boy and come help your mother, will you?"

I could have told you that, I thought about saying, but it would only hurt her feelings, so I kept quiet. I helped her up the stairs and into the back-stage area. This was so cool. It was hard for me to believe my mom could *ever* have been a part of this.

"Here we . . . are," she puffed. "Help me . . . into my chair. . . will you, dear?"

I was afraid she might break it, but being an obedient son, I helped her sit, and amazingly the chair held. She began to fan herself as she looked around, a small smile beginning to form.

"Thank you, David," she said.

"For what?" I asked.

"For taking time out of your busy day to bring me here. It's just as I remembered." She smiled, her eyes all a-sparkle, as if lost in remembrances.

I watched my mom for a while, and noticed for the first time just how pretty she really was. I started to reach out and rub her shoulders, when the floor began to shift beneath my feet.

"Mom? Mom! What's happening?" I gripped the back of her chair, as it began to topple. I wasn't strong enough to keep it upright. Mom screamed as she hit the floor.

"Earth-quake! David! Get under the table, now!" she ordered, but for the first time I cared more about my mom than myself. I pulled the dressing table onto its side, the heavy mirror frame offering some protection. Then the roof fell in. Trapped. I couldn't even reach my cell to call for help.

It seemed like hours we lay there, and prayed. Mom was having some trouble breathing, so I shifted the best I could to give her more room. She began to breathe easier, and I began to relax, just a bit. I was scared, but I couldn't let my mom know it.

"Don't worry, Mom. Someone will be here to rescue us before you know it."

"No, they won't, son. Nobody knows we're here, but us." She groaned as if in severe pain.

"But Dad knows, doesn't he? He'll worry, knowing we came here, and send help."

"I'm afraid not. This trip was a spur-of-the-moment thing. I thought we'd be back long before your dad got home." She shifted position and moaned again.

So this was how it was going to end, just my mom and me, trapped in her old dressing room. This had been her life and now it was going to be her death. Tears formed in the corners of my eyes, but I couldn't let her see them. "Come on, Mom. Let's do what you always do best. Let's sing. Try some of that yodeling you used to do when I was a kid."

I had to get her mind off our situation, and if music would do it, then that's what we'd do. She began to sing, softly at first, but as she sang, she seemed to gain a strength about her, and that tiny cubicle filled with sound. *Now*, I thought, *If we're going to die, we might as well go out with a bang.* Together, we began to belt out every song I think I'd ever known.

* * *

"Hello! Anybody in here? Sounds like a concert outside, so we know you're here somewhere."

"Back here . . . under the dressing table! Please hurry!" I shouted. "My mom needs help, real bad."

"Give us just a minute and we'll have you out-a-there, son."

Well, it took a bit more than a minute, but we did get out, and mom was rushed to the hospital. I went with her. I didn't want her to be alone.

* * *

It's been almost a year now, and graduation is next month. Mom and I became the best of friends after that day. I took her everywhere—concerts, track meets, anything she wanted to do . . . and was able.

I found out something, that day in the hospital, so long ago. Mom really did have a thyroid problem, but what she hadn't told me was, she was also dying of cancer. She passed away last week, but I know she'll be beside me as I walk down that aisle and accept my diploma.

* * *

I'm going to college in the fall. I'm going to teach music. I love you, Mom.

(Alternate ending)

I found out something, that day in the hospital, so long ago. Mom really did have a thyroid problem, and it almost killed her. She's on meds now, and doing pretty good. She'll be at my graduation with bells on, she says. And do you know what else? She's been asked to sing . . . just like old times. She probably never expected to hear me say this, but . . . here goes. "You're My hero, Mom. The best. I love you."

Answers to Red-Eyed Tree Frog puzzle

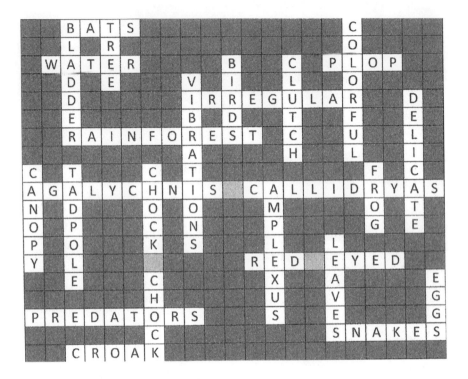

18011052R00110

Made in the USA
Charleston, SC
11 March 2013